BELONGING

About the front cover:

During the last year of the Second World War, when I was four years old, my mother took my sisters, my brother and me from Amsterdam to Murmerwoude, a small village in Friesland, in the northern part of the Netherlands. My father had to stay behind because of his job. The country was occupied by the Nazis, and there was famine in Amsterdam. No one in Murmerwoude could welcome all of us under one roof. So I was separated from my mother and sent to a family whom I did not like. Every morning I sat waiting for my mother on a wooden post in front of the house. At that early age I already experienced the cry for belonging. I didn't know yet that 'my days were inscribed in God's book: they were all decided and set before even I came to be!' That cry for belonging would become longing for Love — a home, finally found in the common life of the Church.

Br Leonard

BELONGING

by

Brother Leonard of Taizé

THE PILGRIM PRESS
New York

First published 1985
by A. R. Mowbray & Co. Ltd,
Saint Thomas House, Becket Street,
Oxford, OX1 1SJ

Library of Congress Cataloging-in-Publication Data

Leonard, of Taizé, Brother, 1940-
    Belonging.

    1. Christian life–Reformed authors.
2. Leonard, of Taizé, Brother, 1940-   . I. Title.
BV4501.2.L448   1985   248.4   85-12388
ISBN 0-8298-0565-6 (pbk.)

The Pilgrim Press, 132 West 31 Street, New York, NY 10001

CONTENTS

A letter of introduction

This book is the reflection of an inner adventure which pilgrims on their lifetime voyage must experience, an adventure that takes place somewhere between their moment of departure and their final destination. The adventure is called 'belonging', and it begins with the sense of gnawing dissatisfaction, isolation, or alienation. Suddenly, you enter a zone of depression. A feeling of void, a frantic fright makes the needle of your compass tremble and lose direction. You lose your luggage, you think you saw San Francisco for the last time, your plane has a delay of seven hours, you don't know any more if it is Thursday or Friday. As if in a parachute you fall to the depths of your existence: what am I doing here? who am I? to whom do I belong? You don't see any stairway on the ground, with its top reaching to the heavens. You feel alone. But in struggling with these questions, the scaffold for interior construction can be set up, ways can be explored — via detours and derailments — to rise towards the heights of God. On the gateway to heaven the Lord stands beside you and says: 'Know that I am with you', 'I will never leave you'.

Belonging was certainly a key word for me during a year of travelling between Taizé and New York, New Hampshire and New Orleans, New Mexico and Newfoundland. Surprising? Is my existence not an existence in community, a life of surrender made possible by the presence of others with whom I share everything in the communion of the Body of Christ? It is, as a gift. On the other hand, at each moment, at each new departure I too have to go through the same litany of questions. Answers do not always abound; trust, however, becomes more and more the consistent foundation amid cloudiness, storms and emergency landings.

1

'What's _your_ business?', my neighbour on the plane asked. We had spoken about delays and disinflation, cities and Cyrano de Bergerac, national policies and Newtonian telescopes. What's my business? Jesus answered with the simplicity of a child: 'I have to be in my Father's house'. I remembered the lady in a Chicago Institute of Spirituality asking me to introduce myself by commenting briefly on the following statement 'I am a galactic cloud — so deep, so involuted, that a light wave would take light years to pass through me . . . and has taken.' My search is, I answered: how to abandon ourselves to the sources of redemption so that our life may be fruitful at the heart of the human family's pilgrimage? And I am convinced that it _is_ fruitful, whether we are capable of abandoning ourselves or not.

But I needed this whole book to say what my business is, today.

The two other Brothers of Taizé with whom I was travelling were sitting up front, one reading his Greek and Latin New Testament, the other plunged in the metropolitan section of the _New York Times_. It was, therefore, in the company of business travellers sitting next to me on the plane that I started to meditate upon my own 'business', and my own longing to belong, between departures and destinations. I thought later that this never-ending search for belonging is not only mine but my neighbour's as well. Even the Church, in its own struggle for belonging, must strive to climb Jacob's ladder.

There was, however, a deeper reason behind my searching. A little time before his recent death, I asked my father, who was an effortlessly giving man, about his view of the future. He answered by using a shibboleth of our Calvinist background: 'Heidelberg Catechism Q and A 1.' I had learned this question and answer in my youth; they had been sealed in my soul, and at that moment I longed for the seal to be opened:

Q. What is your only comfort in life and in death?
A. That I am not my own, but belong — body and soul,

2

in life and in death — to my faithful Saviour Jesus Christ.

The first part of this book is a kind of Way of the Cross. It consists of vignettes of fourteen stations, encounters, situations that touched me and deepened my essential belonging. A traveller through life is tempted by hedonism, self-sufficiency and the evil spirit of isolation. There is salvation in letting yourself be reached by the horrendous suffering people around you struggle with. There is no resurrection elsewhere than on the cross. Only by suffering with those who suffer are we able to abandon ourselves and to recognize the silhouette of Another on the horizon of our destination. But then we are en route, into a sometimes vertiginous, sometimes transfigured world without end. As soon as we let go the tyranny of self and, in stillness, discover the Suffering Servant present in the human family, all the dimensions of belonging, as in reflecting mirrors, break open (Chapter 1).

On our way of belonging we discover the mystery of mutual presence. Self is not everything. We are linked together as human beings much deeper than we think. We belong together as labyrinthal highways connected by intricate passages, as woven webs made up of infinite sets of yarns, as members of the same body. We carry each other. Our whole culture leads us to consider ourselves as an exception, as that potential number one who by his or her performance will transcend the awkward accomplishments of the masses. When I settled in New York in a poor neighbourhood, a man helped me in fixing up the apartment. He donated his time, teaching me something about solidarity but I will never forget his remark when he entered the building and contemplated the horrible shape in which former tenants had left the apartment: 'Leonard, you are a loser'. And I had been so proud of getting rid of some billion cockroaches swimming in the sink and sunbathing with their backs to the wall; of obtaining the cheapest foam mattresses on Canal Street and of transporting them, one under each of my only two arms, on the subway, threatening the other passengers by my unco-ordinated movements; of finding in the local lumber store miles of wood that were to cover ugly looking doorposts, floors and ceilings. The culture wants us to be a winner and to be enthroned on our Olympus. We'd do better to belong to the People of the Beatitudes who receive blessing upon blessing because they espouse a crucified humanity and closely follow Christ himself on his pilgrimage to the final horizon of history. On the road we will make friends with magi and a Madonna, with Elijah and Moses illuminated by the light of life, with unknown Cyreneans forced by the powers of this world to carry the burdens of humanity along with lamenting women and condemned criminals, with two men standing in dazzling dress next to a tomb on a silent morning waiting for Mary Magdalene, Joanna, Mary and the other women, with Peter and John walking past the Beautiful Gate with empty pockets but giving what they had received, and above all with that friend of friends who grew up like a shoot out of dry ground, despised and rejected, acquainted with grief, led to the slaughter but risen, risen indeed, rising to meet us face to face (Chapter 2).

If the mystery of mutual presence is welcomed into the heart of our existence, we are no longer stopped by the red lights of our inhibitions, hesitancies and denials. A sense of responsibility will grow, a decision will be taken and much dynamism will be given to our task to build up the community around us. On every level of life, in families, in cities and on planets, we are called, according to our gifts, to share in a heaven coming down from God, whose dwelling is with humanity. The search for justice, peace and community is part of our sanctification. Our culture cuts up the unity of the human person as if we could separate our individuality from our belonging to neighbours, city, world and cosmos. Prayer, that way of admiring God's love for all, propels us to the very people in whom God's image is present. Presence among neighbours and struggle for justice flow out of prayer and contemplation — non-stop. We are brought to a standstill in our prayer if we don't follow the directions of God's love towards the entire human family, through mission and searching for peace and justice, through intercession and listening, through compassion and the gift of our own life. Christ, said a Church Father centuries ago, lives in the unity of the Father and the Spirit as well as in the least of his brothers and sisters. It is our vocation to give away the gift of belonging we have received, to give and to give up, to abandon and to offer ourselves so that God's abundant life may penetrate hearts and structures, human desires and economic systems (Chapter 3).

What has happened to Christians that even they are no longer able to express their common belonging to the body of Christ? Where has the spirit of reconciliation gone? Churches have multiplied, even increasing their divisions and dissensions, annihilating the very foundations of what the Church is meant to be, a laboratory of peace, a parable of the Kingdom, a sign of contradiction among the nations, a place of welcome amidst the sectarianism and xenophobia of the surrounding society, a community of praise, 'Christ's Body, the completion of Him who Himself completes all things everywhere'. 'Church, become who you are in your depths.' Reconciliation is therefore an essential dimension of our belonging to the One who, in the midst of divisions, calls us to heal his body the Church, and who goes ahead of us in the darkness of the human future into which we are called, with one heart and one soul, to suffer with the suffering. Let us commit ourselves as people of God to enter into a dynamic of unity instead of division, to strive for a revival-in-reconciliation with our seventy times seven churches and so to save the Gospel, given to us when we were dead through the trespasses and sins in which we once walked, following the course of this world. Christ broke down the dividing walls of hostility, he reconciled us to God in one body through the cross. Now we are called to be ambassadors of reconciliation (Eph. 2; 2 Cor.5:20). (Chapter 4)

This book was written at Taizé, France, during the summer of 1984. Beyond the inner circle of the Community of Taizé, some friends were kind enough to read the typescript and to help me with their suggestions. Jon James, from Chaminade College in Honolulu, postponed his week of silence at Taizé in order to work on the pages of this book. Sandy Schwartz, from the University of Chicago, sacrificed part of his vacation with Wordsworth in the French Savoie, carried my book from there all the way to a wedding in New York State and sent it back to me just in time to show it to Sr Mary-Christine Morkovsky, CDP, Ogdensburg, New York. A Eucharist celebrated in the open air with the Wadhams Hall seminarians, while boats on the St Lawrence were passing by as a reminder of the passages in our life, was for me the moment, at the heart of my own search for belonging, to let go of this book and to share it with you.

I

Fourteen Stations on a Way of Belonging

Fourteen situations in which I found myself resounded in me particularly and have accompanied me since then.

I still hear that single shot fired in a motel room, reverberating against the walls of Jackson Square. I still feel how we tried to silence in ourselves its raging echo, in those minutes before 12.01 a.m., deadline of a silenced life.

I still listen to the clergyman who finally found a message of immoderate love at the bottom of the bottle which he had brimmed with doubts and fears. Next to him I see the warden sitting on the bench in the park, with a bulky beam in his eye, and writing on the ground. A word of love consoles whoever is able to express it. I see the renaissance of a man, a clergyman who met demons and angels alike.

As if immobilized on a photograph, I still see that bishop standing, helpless, in front of the picture of his priests and layworkers in Honduras, all assassinated and thrown into a well.

I continue my late evening walks with Mary, Jim and Liz, stars of the night, at the golden gate of New San Francisco.

Every morning I sit at the desk of a Daughter of Charity in the worst ghetto of Chicago, waiting for the twinkling in her clear eyes when the mail with the cheques comes in. Like Ruth she is picking up the corn worldly harvesters have left behind.

I read over and over again the postcard of a nun as a summary of humanity's suffering and transfiguration.

I rehearse every day with those who cannot pray the stammering language of the soul.

Women, mothers of New Orleans, march, weeping, singing, up front in a procession I have joined.

I too want to build bridges with wounded women and men to the other side of the river where they will be welcomed as in their mother's home.

I accompany a hippie in the Pacific from island to island until he finds a cross of hope.

I follow a young woman who alone faces the enemy without weapon, frail as an open hand reaching out for the awful paw of darkness.

I will never forget that 'sister and brother thing' a Black Elder, suddenly moved and brightened, spoke about from his heart of hearts: sisters and brothers of the Cross.

In the Café du Monde I'm called to a new surrender.

For all of them, for all of us, God is our today and our tomorrow. On a way of departures and destinations God is my all and all.

Fourteen stations on a way of belonging. Listen to all those people. We belong together. We belong to the Risen Christ, threshold of human longing.

(i) At midnight the late diners suddenly stood still

'Jesus is condemned to death.'

The late diners in the restaurants around Jackson Square, at first laughing and joking, stand still when they see us immobile in a circle of silence. This evening a demonstration against the death penalty is taking place in front of St Louis Cathedral. Conventioneers, tourists and Orleanians stroll through the French Quarter while a man is scheduled to die

8

by lethal injection at 12.01 a.m. in Texas. How difficult it is to be touched by the sufferings of people far away. As long as a sorrowful event doesn't present itself in our immediate surroundings, creating a danger to our own stability, it is easy for us not to see, not to feel, not to know and to run away from it. We have fun, make plans, chatter, eat and drink, fall asleep while at the same time other human beings are in agony. But now, at the ringing sound of silence, for a moment the people in the square look up as did men and women in Pompeii seeing streams of lava rolling down from Mount Vesuvius.

How to be present to the unseen agony around us? Some convents and monasteries, some lay groups of adoration practise permanent intercessory prayer. I know a movement of young couples whose commitment is to pray one night a month. Some time ago, during a night vigil in Westminster Abbey, I saw a film about urbanites who stay awake or work during the night. Some people have to stay up and make sure that everything functions well, is not damaged, is prepared for the morning when the activities of most people start again. Some of us have to compensate for our absences and indifferences and be present to all the people who at this very minute need help. It is part of the belief in the interdependence and oneness of the human family. To thwart our propensity to live only for ourselves and the harmony of our own world, the uninterrupted prayer of some is necessary to keep the threads of human destiny in its wholeness together. The convent of the Pink Sisters in Philadelphia or the Mexican Carmelite Sisters next to the University of San Francisco are such places of continual prayer, and it is not surprising to notice the deep awareness of the agony in the world one feels in visiting those cloistered convents. There is a mystery in the fact that we live with so many people at the same time, a mystery of simultaneity. At the Stock Exchange you see those round clocks indicating the time in New York, Riyadh, Bangkok and Hong Kong. Even within the North American boundaries

9

one has constantly to calculate the differences in time. What does it mean for the Church, as the place where the life of all the others is cared for and sustained, to be at this very minute in communion with people who are alone, hungry, suffering or who know that in a matter of moments they will be suffocated to death but unable to resist? Deep down in ourselves we know that this simultaneous suffering affects us, although we don't know how.

The late diners, at first laughing and joking, stand still when they see us trying to pray, crying softly, a bit disturbed in our concentration by the coolness of the night and the loud voices echoing under the portal of the cathedral, the length of our silence and the thousand thoughts that divert our attention from Charles Brooks, Jr, an unmarried black man, forty years old, from Fort Worth, Texas. In 1977 along with a co-defendant, he was convicted of the murder of a mechanic and sentenced to death. He was the fourth child in his family, and the youngest by fifteen years. He was very close to his father, who died suddenly of a heart attack when Charles was thirteen. His father's death affected him deeply, and, as he grew older, Brooks had several brushes with the law. In the case at issue, he and the co-defendant kidnapped the mechanic who was accompanying them on a test drive in a used car. They took him to a motel room. There, a single shot was fired, killing the mechanic. At their trials, each man refused to discuss the crime, or to accuse the other of being the actual killer.

One of us has a sheet of information about the action of the Religious Leaders Against the Death Penalty. Noticing a group of observers watching us from a safe distance, he leaves the circle and quietly explains to them the drama that is happening right now. He reads them the text from Romans: 'Beloved, never avenge yourselves, but leave it to the wrath of God; for it is written, "Vengeance is mine, I will repay, says the Lord"' (Romans 12.19). I regret that we are not more numerous and that we are not together in the cathedral to sing the litany of the cross, praying to Christ the prayer of the good thief: 'Jesus, remember me when you come into your Kingdom'. At the end, however, we pray loudly the Our Father, and an episcopal priest says some words, interpreting our helplessness and pointing to that life of Christ in us by which we may take part in his redeeming love. The ecumenical group against the death penalty ministers to death-row inmates and their families as well as to the victims of violent crime; it educates the public about the immorality of capital punishment, and involves as many as possible in prison visitation, correspondence with prisoners, and action to abolish capital punishment and reform the prison system; it works with trial lawyers to provide them with ethical arguments against capital punishment. But somehow we have to find in ourselves as well, every day anew, a space of communion, in those dimensions where the love of our heart rejoins God's own love, in order to be able never to forget in the deepest joy the cross others bear and in the deepest sorrow the light of the Resurrection that will shine over us at that solemn moment of our own death.

(ii) The purity of heart of a drunken clergyman

'Jesus carries his cross.'

A clergyman stood up before all the clergy of his ecclesiastical region and said: 'I want to tell you something about my life, about what I am, and then about how I learned to know who I am.

'I had come to that point in my life where I made a promise to myself: no matter how much I drink during the week, I will not drink on Saturday night, under any circumstances. But I found that even that law which I had imposed upon myself was suddenly shattered.

'On that Saturday night my wife and I had invited some friends for supper. I was really looking forward to their visit. In order to get ready for the party I poured myself three, four scotches, when my wife wasn't looking — just to feel good. When my friends arrived, I took three or four scotches to keep them company before dinner. There was a big bottle of wine on the table. I remember noticing that the others left their glasses half full. But I finished the bottle. After dinner I kept drinking, pouring more scotch. I remember my wife saying "Why won't you come to bed?" "No, honey," I said, "I don't want to yet." I turned the TV on and took another scotch. I tried to concentrate on the movie and I realized that it was absolutely meaningless to me. I picked up a book of theology and kept reading the same paragraph over and over again. I realized I didn't understand a single word. Then my wife called from upstairs: "Honey, are you coming up?" The only reality that mattered to me was sitting there, with that bottle, right next to my armchair. So I finished the bottle that night.

'The next morning I had to go to church and to preach. It was one of the most horrible moments of my life. I approached the pulpit in a kind of shaky numbness. I stood there and I don't know at all what I preached. I had a total blackout when I walked up the altar and tried to meet my God in Holy Communion.

'The following day my senior warden phoned me and told me that we needed to have lunch together. I knew what was going to happen. I knew that the whole wrath of God Almighty was going to come down on me. I knew it but I couldn't turn him down. I took a drink just to get my courage together, bought some sandwiches and met him in the park where we sat down on a bench. We just sat there. He couldn't look at me. And suddenly I realized that his cheeks were wet and that he was sobbing and crying. The only words he could get out were: "I love you so much".

'I could not handle that, these were the last words, this was the last thing in the world I expected. Love broke me down. I became aware of the cleavage between what I am and who I am. The what is: I'm an alcoholic. The who is: I'm a child of God, I'm precious in God's sight. There are lots of people who love me, who are weeping for me and who want to see me whole and free.

'You know, I'm now coming to the point that I'm running around like an evangelist, telling people about the new life. I can tell you, I really believe, there are demons, they take you over, they control you and possess you. I was not my own person, I was possessed and living dead. I was dead and now I am alive, I was lost and now I'm found. There may be such a great difference between the what of what you are and the who of what you are; you may be immature, not whole, wrong, desperately wrong, but that's no reason, no reason at all for a special covenant to come to an end. What a thing it is when that kind of love takes over.'

(iii) A missing link between a bishop and his home in Honduras

'Jesus falls the first time.'

I meet this bishop, a refugee from Honduras. For a whole year he had no job. He thought, 'Where is that collegiality? Nobody was saying anything.' He felt uncomfortable. It's different here from Honduras. There people were persecuted, dying from hunger, without roofs, without beds, children dying, people too poor. Sixty-five thousand campesinos organized a union to combat low wages without benefits, insurance, or vacation. The bishop was very much part of it. And therefore he had to leave in 1976 after working there for thirty years. He had a threat over his head; whoever would kill him would receive twenty thousand dollars. He should be dead now. But he happened to be out of town, collecting funds for projects. In 1975 all his priests, nuns and layworkers — all foreigners except one — were arrested by the military government. Two priests and twelve lay people were killed. Here is a photograph. They were shot and thrown in a deep well, which was then dynamited and covered with grass. The bishop stayed a while in

13

the US. Finally, he went back to Honduras but not to his diocese because of the threats to his life. He couldn't work there any more. What do you do with a dead bishop? The government found it embarrassing, but he decided to leave. He had become a threat to national security for landowners and cattle-owners, all linked with business people around the country. There is no successor in Olancho, Honduras. An empty see, and only two priests for the whole diocese. Bishops have been appointed but it is impossible to work there. 'You have to speak out against injustice, you know. They say, "Stay in the sacristy, you are a bishop, talk about Jesus, talk about love". No, talk about justice too, it's all together. But they don't want to hear the bad things; they want to hear the nice things. In the meantime they're killing my people. I'm supposed to be their shepherd, and don't do nothing.'

Now he is involved in evaluation of parishes, five-year plans of needed spiritual renewal, evangelization, lay ministries, pastoral plans, archdiocesan councils, continuing education programs, social apostolate initiatives, twenty-two priorities in all. When I ask what the main priorities are, he doesn't remember because there are so many, and we laugh. It's different here from Honduras. In Honduras the candidate for the presidency asked him to support his candidacy. The bishop said no. The answer was like the end of the world for the candidate. 'You don't support me? I can give you everything. You ask me for everything, if you want, for churches, for schools. I will do it for you.' The bishop said no. 'I'm sorry, it's the Gospel.' His ringfinger still points to the priests and the lay people on the photograph. His heart beats in Honduras.

Teach us, bishop, to live among the poor. Teach us to learn from Latin America, to renounce our privileges, to raise the awareness of human, economic, political rights both here and there. Teach us the vision of a church that has renounced worldly instruments of power, a church that is poor, missionary, 'paschal', giving away its land, sharing

14

the conditions of life of the poor. Teach us contemplative poverty, hope in the midst of oppression, the life of God in the poor. Teach us the promise of resurrection promised to those who suffer. Contradict a church obsessed with fund raising, success ideology, conformity to the ideals of the surrounding society. Teach us what you saw and suffered during thirty years in Honduras.

Some days later the Franciscan bishop brings some brochures to the house where I am staying. Bishops have that curious custom of handing out photographs of themselves. With the brochures I find one of him, smiling, beautifully silver-haired, dressed up as a Franciscan on the occasion of St Francis' 800th birthday. On the back I read: 'Were this man of peace (St Francis) alive today, he would vehemently condemn the nuclear arms race, militarism, abortion, racism, euthanasia, capital punishment and the futility of the nations that want to be first.' A handwritten PS says: 'Beloved Leonard, may your efforts to seek out hope be successful. No matter what happens Christ is in control. Bishop N.'

(iv) Mary, 16, lives under the Golden Gate Bridge

'Jesus meets his mother.'

I walked one night with the night minister in San Francisco. We met at the entrance of a theatre on Mason Street in the Tenderloin. Some clergy working on the streets dress in jeans, wear long hair and look dirty, making themselves indistinguishable from the fauna of the night; this one, however, was elegantly dressed, a milord of the night whose silvery hair waves in the wind above a fresh and beaming face and a glittering Roman collar. 'Hi! I'm Brother Leonard. I'm here in your fair city and I need a place to stay.' The night minister: 'I see, that's too bad, I have no places of shelter left. What are you going to do tomorrow?'

15

Me: 'Well, I don't know.' He: 'Where do you come from?' Me: 'I just came in from Reno and I'm looking at the country.' He: 'Where are you heading?' Me: 'I thought maybe in a couple of days I'd travel down to Los Angeles.' He: 'Do you have any money?' Me: 'No, my money's all gone.' He: 'Well, gee, that's too bad. Let me see if I can help you.'

Here is a man who is three hundred and sixty-four nights a year on call. He gets over 5,000 calls a year, and his lay volunteers an additional 2,000. Most calls concern housing requests. The other areas of importance deal with religious, marital/family, psychiatric problems, with loneliness, transportation and alcohol problems. Many homeless San Franciscans improvise a home each night. Numbers are put at between five and ten thousand. Ten thousand . . . Old Saint Mary's in Chinatown handles about fifteen beds. The church also has a special facility in the western part of the city that houses about six women and maybe another three or four at a substandard hotel. Women who have been there usually come away and say, 'I never want to stay there again'. But it is shelter, it is off the street and they have a bed. The Gospel Mission has been closed down for a month because they are remodelling it. The Mission will be earthquake proof. The Salvation Army will put up three or four couples every day and Travelers Aid another six people. Hospitality House and St Anthony's have recently opened night-time drop-in centres, with one hundred and twenty spaces. The others total some two hundred and twenty-five. But 10,000 . . .

And the others? Some sleep in doorways, in the park underneath the freeway, in the hedges at the entrance of the freeway, under the bridge, wherever. The runaways on Polk Street look for a friend to go home with. At Hospitality House eighty men are allowed to come in at 11 p.m., but there are no blankets, no cots and it is forbidden to bring a sleeping bag or a bed roll. The first ones get a chair; everybody else ends up on the floor. St Anthony's takes thirty

16

women, or children up to the age of eighteen. If you are number thirty-one, you are on the street. The night minister has some limited space at the YMCA on Turk Street. There, for instance, he will house a battered woman. If someone calls from the women's shelter or from the Sexual Trauma Center needing a place for a woman who has been raped or battered, he will have a bed for her. He saves accommodation for families with children, especially small children. He can use any vacant room in the Y for free, nine hundred people a year, which means for the night ministry a saving of fifteen thousand dollars.

The night minister's beeper calls him to a bar. I walk to St Anthony's. There the Franciscans serve eighteen hundred meals a day. A clinic serves three hundred people a week, free. The transients have put their heads on the table and gone to sleep. Thirty-five agencies, the Central City Shelter Network, met today to press City Hall to begin dealing with the issue and to fund additional shelters. In New York City, which has an estimated 36,000 homeless, the City only began dealing with the problem when a lawsuit was brought against them and they lost. Here they want to obtain housing before the winter. Last year a few people died of hypothermia; they lost their body heat and died, unnecessarily, from the cold and the rain in a city full of vacant hotels and empty buildings.

I run into Mary, 16. She lives under the bridge. I'm ashamed of my egoism, the protection of my schedule, ashamed of my tiredness, of my travelling and leaving, of my spectator attitude. Because here is Mary who has the human right of warmth and happiness, of a house, of a garden, of an angel and of great things, of shepherds and of gold, frankincense and myrrh. 'We had a tent and couch. Basically, half my family was under there and it was pretty neat, I thought. So I wasn't scared 'cause they were around — my mother, my brother, his girlfriend, my mom's boyfriend, so it was pretty neat. She got cut off Social Security and she's really disabled, she's got a pin in her leg, now

17

she's back on GA. She can do no work. We had a little firepit, we'd get buckets of water from the gas station, it was like camping out in a regular campground. We had a couch and stuff, it was pretty neat.' Even under the Golden Gate Bridge, there where the sun goes down, at the end of the rainbow, a star goes ahead of a neat family. It is the same star that shines over Liz who was kicked out of her home in Wyoming and became a prostitute. When her stepmother died, she went home for the funeral and tried to patch things up with her father. But her father kicked her out again. Now she is pregnant and is still a prostitute. The same star accompanies Jim, 26, who came to the city three days ago. He moves about all the time, three months here, two months there. Then he finds a lover for a couple of months, finds a job but gets fired. He also has a severe medical problem. Clothes on his back, stolen from department stores, taking the bus with the change that was left as a tip for a waiter, he goes from place to place. For the last three days he went to a bar. Tonight he called the night minister for suicide prevention. What had happened? Jim was hustling drinks. He never bought himself a drink. Tonight he asked the bartender for a dime to make a call. The bartender overheard the conversation and told everybody that the night minister would come. The night minister met Jim at the far end of the bar where he was all by himself, rejected by all.

That star didn't stop in Bethlehem. Mary, Jim and Liz under the Golden Gate Bridge do know what it would be like to be free, delivered, safe, rescued, risen. They belong to a family of people who in the Kingdom will need neither stars nor lamps to enter into New San Francisco through its golden gate but will walk in front of us as queens and kings.

(v) Sister Sisyphus

'Simon helps carry the cross.'

She gets the morning mail and looks first for the checks. How to keep the place going with a day-care centre for four hundred and sixty-five children, keep the electric lights on and pay salaries for one hundred and five staff people, all from the neighbourhood, who work at Marillac House? The Daughters of Charity in Chicago have one settlement house on the Northside serving Spanish, white, Oriental, black, middle-class and poor people, and this one, Marillac House, on West Jackson Boulevard, in the heart of a densely populated black community. The sister has the clear eyes and the realistic determination of her Dutch ancestry.

In Chicago the old Calvinist wisdom reigns: if you are poor, you probably deserve it. But the sister says there are many rich who are slobs, bums, lazy types, alcoholics. She has worked on the Westside for fifteen years and knows that the poor are not perfect. But for her, poverty is 'a kind of a system problem'; there are no jobs, no training, no good education. She tries to push people and to help them to maximize their potential, to live their own lives so that they are able to stand on their own feet and use their own resources to deal with life. But poverty is only an individual problem in a few cases, such as when it is a result of serious drug or alcohol problems. Thousands and thousands of blacks have no jobs, have no money to turn the heat on, live in houses that are falling apart. 'Capitalism is not very Christian; people fall by the wayside,' she says.

The house is open from 7 a.m. until 9.30 p.m., since, in addition to day care, there are after-school programmes, recreation for teens, a food pantry, an emergency relief program, outreach to the elderly, and so forth. For the safety of the building and as a witness, the sisters live in the building. The leading cause of death for young blacks up to the age of thirty is murder. Gangs, violence, drugs,

19

unemployment — everybody on the Westside will show it and speak about it. Extreme poverty is no friend of personal growth, family life, or religion. People must have enough to eat, to clothe themselves, to have some quiet and some sense of job-security. Residential segregation in Chicago is the key to all the differences in school, in city services, in the churches. At least the little children in Marillac House who enter the centre frightened relax after six weeks, eat, make friends, learn skills and move around more freely.

St Vincent de Paul called the poor 'our lords and masters', and that is what I think of as I listen to the sister and walk with her through Marillac House. People working among the poor are like dungbeetles, rolling huge burdens ceaselessly up the hill, persevering like Sisyphus: they never have finished. But amidst all the storms of human life the sister is a lighthouse, sending out signals of courage and of a love beyond human imagination. No organization other than the Church can urge women and men to commit themselves in the same way, so totally. Going from place to place I have this privilege of meeting people who give their lives because of 'the love of Jesus crucified'.

(vi) A woman's pilgrimage

'Veronica wipes the face of Jesus.'

One hundred words on a postcard: 'Our prayer in the cathedral had special meaning for me. It helped heal an old wound. Twelve years ago I came to this city as a student. The night after I arrived I was picked up, beaten and raped. I thought I would be killed. I didn't know the area at all but remembered it was behind a Greyhound bus station. When I arrived at the cathedral on Sunday and saw the same bus station across the street, I could recall the terror of that night. How good it was to be there this time on a pilgrimage of peace and reconciliation.'

(vii) Even a mantis prays

'Jesus falls the second time.'

A church without prayer? In a city where young adults told me they came to pray 'to search for the infinite God' whom they hadn't found in denominations? In San Francisco where a minister warns me that the God of the denominations is a God of law and the God of ecumenism is issue-centred and not 'love-centred'? Where everybody agrees that young people are looking for a God who cares, looking for a gospel that makes sense on a day-to-day basis in their lives? They would go for that gospel, whatever denominational label it may have. Would the cults be so successful if they didn't offer some answer to people who have a yearning for some spiritual transcendent experience but who have not been given the incentive to conduct a spiritual life by churches, families, schools? All of a sudden they are given a framework and they go for it. A church without prayer? People travel to St Columba's in Inverness every Sunday to find prayer. St Boniface in the Tenderloin area recently instituted daily vespers because people working in the area asked for it.

Glide Memorial Church has a unique physiognomy. A Methodist Church? Everybody praises its great ministry while being perplexed by its avoidance of any language about God. The church stands between a Hilton, a Ramada Inn, a Holiday Inn, and the Tenderloin neighbourhood with its streetpeople and its very poor housing conditions. When the Ramada Inn wanted to build, Glide insisted that the city should not grant the developers a permit to build unless they would put something back into the community. They suggested that they contribute to a community fund to develop housing for the poor, for the elderly and those on fixed incomes. It is part of Glide's work to influence the city structures, primarily the businesses that go into the area solely to make profit, to influence them to exercise some social concern. Working together with the construction

21

unions, they also make sure that people from the neighbourhood are able to participate.

At the entrance to the church people are waiting for a meal. From Monday to Friday all those who are waiting to get on general assistance plus anybody who is hungry receive an evening meal; in addition, those in the first category — a hundred to a hundred and twenty people — get breakfast and lunch seven days a week. In the evening there are six or seven hundred people. Street people are present on Sunday morning as well. They may speak up or shout; the minister will adjust to their presence and engage in conversation right in the middle of the sermon. The folks from the streets feel very much at home with the middle-class members and the singles. Glide has a wide variety of ages, life-styles, ethnic groups and classes. A good number of them are single parents and their children have gone through very difficult times. Gays and lesbians feel very much at home. Glide has no specialized ministry for them; basically they are part of the total ongoing programme.

Why does it go so well in this church? One reason why people come to Glide is the recognition that regardless of who they are, of what their life-style, of what their class, they will be very much accepted. In other churches — local churches — the group that sets policy often feels threatened by any sort of change, and they make decisions despite the pastor who is always trying to open things up. The board of trustees at Glide is not elected by the local church but by the Annual Conference, so the trustees and the staff set policy. Certainly the main policy is that this is a church for all people. The celebrations are very appealing. The choir is mixed, multi-generational, multi-ethnic, and the music is very contemporary. They have a four-piece jazz band that provides the music. Instead of using song books or hymn notes, they project onto the front wall all the words of their songs. Along with the lyrics they also project pictures of life in the city. A group of volunteers up in the balcony handles the light show with a whole assortment of pictures that enhance the celebration. There is an open, free liturgical style, strong preaching, but above all an emphasis on community. From the time that people walk in they try to create that spirit, a sense of unity and community. Their present focus is ministering to the poor and those at the very bottom of the social scale, those who have been excluded or marginalized by society.

They don't say very much about their Methodist denomination. Glide has devised their own membership commitments: a commitment to change the world, to change the traditional church, to reach out to all people: the young, the old, all ethnic minorities, the poor, homosexuals. They are also committed to the three Cs: to be a caring, compassionate and concerned community. And the C of Christian? Glide wants to stay clear of traditional expressions because many of its members have been turned off by the church. They experience a spiritual community they haven't experienced in other churches. The spiritual dimensions are not understood as a relationship to God — an abstraction, they would say — but in relating to the spiritual in the other. Something emerges out of that caring and sharing in depth with another person, and that something is powerful and spiritual. Spirituality is for them not the search for transcendence, the longing for God expressed through meditation, prayer and contemplation. Nor is it one's relationship with God that once having taken place will cause everything else to fall into place, or an emphasis on the other-worldly or one's relationship to the unknown. It is the relationship of people to the concrete issues of our world here and now and with other human beings.

There is dance, singing, silence; there are skits, plays, dramas. Preaching of course. But no prayer . . . A church without prayer?

Everywhere else among Methodists, at the yearly covenant service in which people take upon themselves 'the yoke of Christ', 'the yoke of obedience', the minister shall say: '. . . Let us now, in sincere dependence on His grace and trusting in His promises, yield ourselves anew to Him, meekly kneeling upon our knees.' Then follows a prayer after which all the people join in one of the most beautiful prayers of the Christian tradition written by Wesley himself (This prayer sounds almost literally like the one at the end of the Spiritual Exercises of St Ignatius: 'Take, Lord, and receive all my liberty, my memory and all my will, all I have and possess. You gave it to me: I give it back to you, Lord. All is yours, do with it what you want. Give me your love and your grace; they will be enough for me'):

'I am no longer my own, but Thine. Put me to what Thou wilt, rank me with whom Thou wilt; put me to doing, put me to suffering; let me be employed for Thee or laid aside for Thee, exalted for Thee or brought low for Thee; let me be full, let me be empty; let me have all things, let me have nothing; I freely and heartily yield all things to Thy pleasure and disposal . . .'

(viii) Weeping women

'Jesus speaks to the women.'

Someone should write a history of suffering in New Orleans. Suffering is characteristic of this city. Everywhere New Orleans is known as a music town, a resort place, a tourist attraction, and, it is true, all the suffering has not apparently created depression; somehow, in this climate, with the richness of their diversity, people survived. Sweet Emma survived at Preservation Hall playing piano with the serenity of her eighty years of experience accompanying the old Dixieland melodies. Dressed as a New Orleans Cardinal in red chasubles kept together by a yellow life-belt, leaning towards the left of the piano, moved by musical trance, she seemed to listen to the consummated sonority of the dark tones, unless her attitude was provoked by tiredness due to the late hour. But do the tunes, the dances and the masks forget the city's veils and the inaudible mourning? Perhaps the wailing that one hears throughout New Orleans is not heard.

Someone should write about St Jude, the burial church. During epidemics hundreds of people died each day. It was impossible to hold requiem masses or special celebrations. Horse-drawn carts went through the streets as if they were selling vegetables, and the men on the cart would ask: any dead today? People could have lost up to three or four members of their family; they would wrap them up in sheets and pile them up on the wagon. The priest would give a general blessing of the bodies and they would be buried in the cemeteries called St Louis number one, two and three. Most of the tombs were above ground. The reason is that many parts of the city are far below sea-level. If you dig three feet you come to water. Trying to dig six feet to bury a body you would dig a well. It made underground burial very difficult. It was a very gruesome thing. As soon as any rain would come, the corpses would be scattered all over. They tried at one time to bore holes in the wooden caskets and to put bricks and big stones in them so that the coffins would settle. But it didn't work. Therefore the idea of building 'ovens' above the ground was finally accepted. Lamenting women, mothers of New Orleans . . .

Mourning was something very realistic. If an immediate member of the family died, all the other members — wife, mother, father and close family — discarded all coloured clothing and wore only black — hats, stockings, shoes. The women had huge mourning veils. If their husbands died, the women had a special kind of veil, widows' veils with very big black laces that completely covered the widows' faces. They wore that to the funeral. If the women worked, they used thinner veils for three months. Afterwards, the veils would go back over their head and not cover their faces any more. They would, however, still wear black dresses and black shoes. The deep mourning lasted one whole year. The second mourning dress consisted of black and white material. The women would wear white dresses trimmed

25

with black, or black dresses trimmed with white. If the men didn't have a black suit, they would cut out a piece of material from the sleeve of their jacket, five inches long, two inches wide, and insert a black band. The tragedy of these mourning rites was that invariably every year somebody was dead in those very large families of six to ten children. Often women never wore anything else but black. Lamenting women, mothers of New Orleans . . .

Before the days of the funeral parlours the undertaker came to your home to embalm the body and lay it out in the front room of the house. Neighbours had made the burial clothes and the shrouds. Later the undertaker would come back to place the body in the coffin. If it were someone important, the family would keep the body at home three or four days. If you were an ordinary member of the community, you would be buried the same day. In the Catholic community the dead were buried the next day. Many people walked in the funeral procession. The priest would sit in the first carriage, the family in the second, sometimes the third, and all the rest of the community would walk behind. Many lay-societies existed; their names emulated all kinds of virtues, for instance Les Dames et Demoiselles du Silence (Ladies of Silence). As a member you contributed five or ten cents a week. Every month there was a meeting with friends, with food and a party. If you got sick, the 'sick committee' would visit you. Salaries were so poor that it was impossible to save money for a funeral (the established insurance companies did not insure black people), so the societies took care of that. The 'burial committee' took care of the wake, brought coffee and beignets. People sat around all night long, reminisced, talked, drank coffee, cooked food. The fraternity members came to the wake and played music. Lamenting women, mothers of New Orleans, you sang from the heart of sorrow to God, and jubilation sprang up.

Someone should write about the women in the St Thomas housing project, have them describe their lives, have them teach us about welfare, criminal justice, health care, and education. About what makes a person go on welfare and how it feels to be on welfare. About what it is like to raise a family in public housing. About what are schooling, health care, employment opportunities, or prisons from the perspective of the poor. About what poverty does to a family. About what carries a person through. Right now a strike is going on. Over a hundred thousand dollars in rental fees have been withheld as residents protest the unlivable conditions in the project as well as the increasing utility rates. Five hundred people, that is to say one-third of the residents, are taking part in the strike. The people are beset by multiple pressures and their human concerns make them so disturbed that normally they can't be expected to take on responsibilities at a neighbourhood level. But at times, even they get angry because of the neglect of the buildings that are their homes, some organization occurs. Today is a high; people are taking charge and on this very evening three people from the community, untrained and uneducated, are talking on the phone, negotiating with lawyers and housing authorities. And tomorrow? Will the organization fall apart again? Many people who had never had to ask for assistance are coming to direct services desks, while others who have come before now come more frequently, desperate and in great need. Food stamps were cut; low-income energy assistance funding was cut; Aid to Families with Dependent Children and Supplemental Security Income benefits were cut. Cuts in funding for public housing have caused an increase in rent. Welfare recipients have to fill out frequent reports. Computer foulups, case-worker errors, delays in mail delivery have caused some to be dropped from the rolls, and reapplication takes months.

Women, mothers of New Orleans . . . In 1979 there were 3,228 pre-school children with school-age mothers. One of eight females from 15 to 19 years old was pregnant. Teenage mothers are responsible for 30 per cent of the child abuse cases. The local infant mortality rate is 20.3 out of 1,000 births. Economically, 22.3 per cent of New Orleans households in general fall below the poverty level.

Someone should write a history of suffering, starting with the trip over from Europe, with the raging yellow fever, the incredible amount of human suffering, especially of the blacks from Africa and the West-Indies living in the swamps who were forced over the centuries to conquer this place on the Mississippi and to obtain its wealth. It was a swampland. The first settlements were difficult to reach; it was only possible to get to them at certain times of the year. The land was so vast in the western section of Louisiana that people coming home on Sunday night from a party would get lost and would never be seen again. Hurricanes swept the country at regular intervals. Artificial levees had to be built to master the Nile of New France that made its serpentine way to the west of the Isle of New Orleans. A geographer summarizes what was wrong with the site: the oldest part of the city is built on natural levees, just above sea-level; behind the city was a half-flooded swamp; foundation material consisted of compacted clays, seventy feet at least below the surface; during floods crevasses in the natural levees, the only avenues in the city, made access to the outside impossible; no nearby hinterland; mud and sandbars at the entrances of the Mississippi; the sinking of the city . . . A place of suffering with the Mardi Gras as a travesty of daily life, working all year round designing costumes and masks, fleeing an unlivable life.

Someone should keep humanity's suffering in the palm of his hand. Someone should write the lives of women, mothers of New Orleans, in the book of the living. Words that are true and can be trusted. Write this: God will wipe away all tears from their eyes.

(ix) Bridge building

'Jesus falls the third time.'

Bridge Building is a place in San Francisco, near Golden Gate Park. A priest lives there. The house is tastefully arranged, clean, silent, warm and friendly. It is a place of urban retreat, especially for those who don't feel at ease in parishes or have been excluded or wounded by the church — technically called 'the alienated', although all the others are alienated as well, being deprived of their visions and dreams.

There are, of course, parishes in San Francisco where staff people are working very well together and are trying to innovate liturgies and to devise pastoral forms that are really adapted to the needs of the people, even if the structure is oftentimes unwieldy, old and inflexible. Very good things are happening. In spite of this, the overall image is that the parish does not change, has not renewed itself, is not able to include people who don't respond exactly to the image of family-minded middle-class or immigrant parishioners. Bridge Building's question is: Why would the people who don't feel attracted to the parish for whatever reason not gather together and do something else? Many people perceive some kind of inner call that they need to take seriously but find no avenue to express that call. They would like to do something more with their life but don't find themselves at ease with any church to express that call and find support for it. Bridge Building offers people encouragement to take seriously that voice they hear within them: Yes, go forward. Do something with your life. In most cases those ministries will be lived out alongside or even outside of the parish. Could the parishes in the future not become able to take more seriously the people who minister outside of their structures, to confirm them and to recognize those already existing ministries?

When the priest began this ministry of bridge building some years ago, his desire was to find ways to help people who were feeling cut off from the Christian community and yet felt a call to follow the Gospel or to live out their spiritual lives, who had stepped away from the community for one reason or another, then felt the call to go back and yet felt very uncomfortable in doing so. His first task has been to tell people not to feel guilty about their orientations. Some acknowledged feeling as close to Protestant Christians as they did to Catholic Christians; others were making choices that would alienate them from others. The priest deals in particular with young adults. It is often difficult for a young single person to participate in a parish that is mainly oriented to families. He is in touch with people who have many serious questions concerning a deeper spiritual life, questions that the parish very often does not address. The parishes don't offer small forums for single people to get together and exchange their experiences. These young adults want to take charge of their own life, they have a sense of call but they think they have to give this up when they go to the parish, to put their lives in the hands of the pastor and the hands of the people. Even though it may not exist, the image many have of the parish is the authority structure, the oppressive rigidity. Catholics especially seem caught up in the conviction that somebody else has to make your decisions, or at least that you have to clear your ideas with somebody before pushing ahead.

Women show an increasing amount of anger at the fact that the parish is male- and clergy-dominated. Even women religious, rather conservative in their outlook, often get angry when they sit down to talk about the church. They get angry particularly at priests they have worked with, even if it may not be because of the priest's personal fault but because of the patterns that have developed. Priests who want to break out of those structures find it almost too difficult to achieve because of the amount of work entailed, the expectations they have to meet, the routine in which they are caught up. How to discern ways for the future beyond the tensions, the uneasiness or anger of young adults or women religious concerning the church — and vice versa perhaps? Bridge Building, as its name says, tries to develop forms of bridging, to bridge the gaps that wouldn't be bridged otherwise, to offer a forum where people can come and share their experiences, where they can begin to work some things out and where they are affirmed rather than denied, a forum also where people can sense a different presence of the Church. Parish is not the only way for the church to be.

The priest himself doesn't practise underground liturgies. With women who are finding it increasingly difficult to attend the Eucharist, he would rather explore other kinds of worship together where it is not necessary to make the same role definitions that prevail in the institutional church. The Archbishop has been very supportive, and there is a deep awareness in the church of San Francisco of the problems of the alienated — young adults, women, divorced and separated, the gay and lesbian population. The priest worked first in San Mateo in adult education for about ten years, out of a small store-front centre. Increasingly, he found that, as the seventies went on, more and more people he was able to contact were drifting away from parishes and were having difficulty with parishes for a variety of reasons. Thinking about the Bridge Building house, he wanted a clear relationship with the diocese so that in meeting people wounded by the church he could say: We can create a different kind of presence that is truly a Catholic presence. He thinks there is a need for vision. 'I think the biggest felt need both of the people, and I'm sure of the bishop too, is that we need a common vision. We need an image of the Church that fits the reality of our lives.'

He does not have enough time for bridge building both ways, doing advocacy to the diocese about concerns that the diocese doesn't want to hear yet. He wants rather to offer some models for people to relate to; if the models work, one day someone will say: maybe that is a form worth taking seriously. Would it be possible in the future for women to be included on an equal basis in directing ministries they fulfil? In the archdiocese people talk more and more about shared responsibility in decision-making. Will it be possible in the congregations to have people from more heterogeneous backgrounds relating to one another so that parishes become more representative of the content of the city which has an extremely diverse population, even if some of them don't think like the others? The bridge-building metaphor fits church situations where people who have different points of view don't allow one another to speak; they have to learn to listen more and to know that out of bridge-building emerges reconciliation as a manifestation of the Spirit.

(x) A Pacific pilgrimage

'Jesus is stripped of his clothes.'

We met on the promenade in Half Moon Bay, south of San Francisco, between the 'Crab Cottage' and a noisy jazz club. I was looking across the ocean in the direction of Japan, trying to imagine what our Brothers of Taizé out there could be doing at that very moment. Some young people were horseback riding on the beach. But then this couple, like a wave of light, came up to me. She was Japanese–American, he was from Belgium. They were living in a tiny trailer, peeping through the little bay window into the immensity of the Pacific Ocean. Inside the trailer we talked as we sat on rugs, looking at an icon of Christ, sharing our faith as if we had discovered it yesterday as an utmost secret. The Belgian took me on a pilgrimage across the Pacific in a few hours' time. Risks taken, dangers overcome, solitude and suffering transfigured, seemed present in the light of his eyes, beaming like a floating-beacon into the inner ocean of our searching.

Ten years ago he left Europe as an angry young man, in revolt against an impenetrable society, a hypocritical Church and the claws of an indiscriminate anxiety. At twenty he wanted to start his life anew, in an unspoiled world without dead ends. At the centre of an island in the north of New Zealand, while working in the forest for three years, all his anxiety that had been translating itself into asthmatic attacks came to a paroxysm. He couldn't sleep any more, or stand on his feet, he felt abandoned, far away from home, hemmed in, ill and lost. Like other hippies he had tried the Oriental way, initiated himself into the secrets of transcendental meditation, listened to the best gurus, practised all kinds of yoga exercises, travelled on a motor-cycle up and down the islands which make up New Zealand in a desperate search for inner peace. But then he opened the small New Testament in French somebody had given to him, and read: 'Peace is my gift to you, my own peace, such as the world cannot give. Set your troubled hearts at rest, and banish your fears.' Alone in his little room he felt restored in his soul and body by the freshness of Christ's words. He discovered that he had rejected indeed the ecclesiastical system but that Christ was branded in the depths of his existence.

And his pilgrimage started there. On the ocean, north of Auckland, he started to walk again. Every morning he walked into the sea, searching for calm, power and healing. He couldn't work any more; he was ill but he walked into the sea on the rhythm of the Our Father. In the evening, on the beach, he soaked in the air and asked God to help him. His Christian faith, originally Catholic, was now personal but very much centred on himself. He wanted to discover some wisdom and first of all peace. He had no notion of belonging to a community, no idea of being called to a service. In this individualistic state of mind he decided to travel for a whole year: to the New Hebrides, the Fiji Islands, the Solomon Islands.

On one of the Fiji Islands from time to time he entered a Catholic church where a priest passed through once a week. Missionaries have shared the Pacific: Congregationalists went to Hawaii, Presbyterians to the New Hebrides,

Methodists to the Fiji Islands and Tonga. But Methodism did not attract the Belgian hippie, he didn't like the hymns and their militaristic rhythms. He needed more mysticism. He was only happy in a Catholic setting. There he prayed, there he knelt, there he received the Eucharist. At the same time he admired the missionary dynamism of the Protestants. On an island of the New Hebrides he was welcomed by a Presbyterian minister; in Brisbane, Australia, by a Baptist minister; in the north of Borneo a Christian from the Philippines helped him with five dollars in a crucial moment and he discerned in that gesture a confirmation of God's love for him. His faith became more and more 'Protestant', and vertical: God and me, and you, and you. But by now he had discovered a gift to speak about his faith to others; as soon as he had read a passage in the Bible, he ran to his neighbours to share what he had found.

After many detours he settled with his wife in Half Moon Bay and became a missionary among the Mexican farmworkers in California. He worked out of a Hispanic Baptist Church in the Mission District of San Francisco. He started Bible studies in the barracks on the ranches where the *campesinos* lived. Although they called him and his friends '*los alleluias*' and remained reticent because of their at least traditional Catholic affiliation, his voluntary preaching was noted by the church leaders, and their Mission Board hired him. In San Jose, in the valley around Fresno, and in the centre of Mexico he wrote reports about possibilities of starting a Hispanic ministry. His title became 'church planter'. In the meantime he had signed his missionary commitment at a national congress. Only one problem bothered him: his converts had been Catholic; Protestant cells in Mexico alienated Catholics from their own Church; his preaching had to become polemical ('not the statues but the living God'!) and self-righteous. He loved to pray, to read his Bible, to rediscover the simple faith of the first Christians, to be an evangelist. He found Catholicism bizarre, ritualistic, pagan. But for him to become a successful church planter, to build up a system outside of Catholicism, to bring in people in order to justify his own work before the Mission Board, to number the people he conquered as a missionary's trophy and harvest, to feel like a Protestant spy who was infiltrating himself among the Catholics in order to convert them — all this was going too far. He suffered from the painful divisions among the Churches. He became thirsty for the sources beyond divisions and dissensions. Had he accepted the job because he needed to work, to earn money for his family? Why did he earn much more than the farmworkers with their families of twelve children? Far from having to justify the budget, he wanted the Gospel to be free, and for himself to take a real risk with Christ. More and more he said to the people he evangelized: Become who you are. Finally he became a farmworker himself.

Today he belongs to both traditions. He loves the freedom and the dynamism of the Protestant churches but the Catholic Eucharist nourishes him. No Church, he says, will satisfy him entirely; he belongs to all of them. In contemplation and meditative prayer he feels himself at home, but Catholics will not send him on the road for the mission of the world. He needs both traditions. In Hawaii where he now lives with his family he found, patiently, ways to reconcile in himself both traditions. He has suffered much, and he still suffers from the Church. Working with the Asian refugees he has found a way of serving, but he hopes that the Lord will open a door so that he may live out fully his missionary commitment, being Catholic and Protestant at the same time. Each Friday, together with friends, he goes with a cross from church to church in Honolulu, often among the young Laotians, inviting people from all directions and walks of life to pray together. It is the cross of his own odyssey but it is also a cross of reconciliation.

(xi) 'On behalf of all those who are longing for life'

'Jesus is nailed on the cross.'

During a 'pilgrimage of reconciliation' in Philadelphia, all the participants travelled to places of hope and reconciliation. Hosts shared their reasons for hopefulness in their community. Each host had a unique perspective in matters that ranged from individual social services and community organization to neighbourhood preservation and church-related social agencies. During the time of preparation for the pilgrimage people had been sought who minister to the poorest of the poor or who witness for peace in their neighbourhood, bring racial reconciliation, work to end unemployment or proclaim the Gospel in new and fresh ways, ways of the Spirit. Each participant received a sheet of paper, with the name of a neighbourhood, for instance 'Germantown', and a schedule:

'2.00 Arrive at First United Methodist Church of Germantown.

2.00–2.30 Welcome and introduction to the neighbourhood.

2.30–2.45 Travel to places of hope and reconciliation.

Group I: Upper Germantown.

Bread and Joy — Afterschool Programme at 529 E. High — Community Renewal of Germantown — Unit Block of East Walnut Lane — Northwest Interfaith Movement.

Group II: Lower Germantown.

Covenant House Health Services — Inn Dwelling — Boarding Home

3.30–4.45 Time for Visiting.

4.45–5.00 Travel to St Vincent's Rectory . . .'

Before leaving, all participants prayed a litany to begin their neighbourhood visits: 'Leader: Let us go forth into the new seasons of our lives. Others: We go forth into growing and changing and living.'

I was assigned to St Vincent's and found myself sitting in the sacristy facing a frail young woman who was supposed to tell me her story. She was allowed access to the sacristy because she had co-ordinated religious education in the parish until her time was more and more spent with a peace group. Clearly, this group's ministry absorbed her, and a fire of the Spirit spoke through her in the stuffiness of the sacristy. A few people against the world, a resistance group acting 'on behalf of all those who are longing for life' — Christianity lives again, on fire. Out of the life they share as community, out of their prayer and celebration, they soon felt themselves called to act in some symbolic fashion, in particular against nuclear weapons. Often this even took the form of breaking some civil laws. Recently, this woman was arrested with four other members of the Brandywine Peace Community, at General Electric's Space Center in Valley Forge, Pa., after they sealed off the building's main entrance by chaining themselves between two sets of vestibule doors. They purposely shed their own blood. They had been between the doors for about thirty minutes before security guards ripped off the chained handles. The space centre — the US fourth largest war contractor — produces the nuclear Defense Satellite Ccmmunications System. While locked between the doors, they celebrated the Eucharist as a remembrance of Christ 'crucified today by nuclear warmaking'.

Her community is named after the Brandywine battlefield, with some irony, because they see themselves as an alternative to the warrior response to conflict and as non-violent people. Everything they do is intensified by the risks they take and by the persecution they undergo, and emanates from their life of prayer together. People who know the cost of living out the Gospel, open up through praying together, acting together in small ways first, until they come to the point that they are willing to say: 'I put my life on the line, I want to give over my life to what we confess in our liturgy!' According to the woman in the sacristy,

37

people of faith have to assert their belief in the power of love in all the places where idols dwell, wherever that may be, but particularly in the nuclear weapons facilities. Because there originates so much of the evil that permeates the world.

So they chained the doors to say that these doors should not be opened. They celebrated the Eucharist for Christ crucified. They shed their own blood as a sign of that other Blood shed for all. They walked into a building like through the Red Sea as a sign of resurrected hope that they hold up against death and destruction.

There are times when risks we take, words we say, scandals we provoke have to be equal to the evil we confront. A frail young woman faces the enemy, her only weapon her open hands. Jail her, kill her, she can't be stopped — like all those people who are committed and ready to give over their lives, gathering together to celebrate the oneness of the human family which Christ brings.

(xii) A Black Elder crowned by a Ukrainian dome

'Jesus dies on the cross.'

Take the trolley in Philadelphia (or the bus if the trolley is not running) north of 5th Street to Thompson Street. Walk west on Thompson Street to 7th Street. Temple United Presbyterian Church is on the corner of 7th and Thompson Streets. A World War II bombed-out city? The slum is worse than Mathare Valley in Nairobi. The struggle in the community is the struggle between life and death. Here children do not have a childhood. They become little old men and women in the survive-a-day world. Amtrak trains pass by North Central Philadelphia's Ludlow Community, but it is the most forgotten and neglected area of the city. Walk around if you dare and ask for the Elder. Give my greetings to Temple Church. You will scarcely understand the Elder's broken voice but now and then you will pick up a word of life, words that suddenly burst out of toothless mumbling and brainless blackouts. Each time it will be a little epiphany. You will be sitting at the table. The windows are steamed up. A curtain of rain hangs as a drapery outside the window. The Ukrainian cupola of the cathedral next door fills the wide window as a shadow of the Most High, as a pillar of cloud just parked in the air for the length of a conversation. The Elder on his kitchen chair makes you think of Van Gogh's little old man, sitting by the fire, with his head bowed forward on his fists, at Eternity's Gate. Van Gogh writes to his brother: 'This is far from theology, simply the fact that the poorest little woodcutter or peasant on the heath or miner can have moments of emotion and inspiration which give him a feeling of an eternal home, and of being close to it.' The Elder, former miner from West Virginia, ravaged by life but illumined by the light of another world, seems in these moments of emotion and inspiration to wear the crown of the Ukrainian dome.

Yes, Temple Church has changed a lot; it has its ups and downs. It grows and then all at once it declines. Everything was going along pretty well, but through some kind of misunderstanding a young group, a little singing group had problems, and then the Reverend said something to them, and they all left. The Elder sees the choir coming back one day. He has been Elder for thirteen years. First he had gone to a Methodist Church on 7th and Oxford; later he went to the Catholic Church, because some lady wanted him to go with her. He took the four classes which are a prerequisite for becoming a member there. But then he had this terrible accident that hurt his back in 1968. The Reverend from Temple Church came to visit him. He told him that whenever he was able he'd come to his church. And when he went, he began to like it and became a member. Later on he was asked to be an Elder. He asked for some time to think it over. He went to the hospital to visit the Reverend, told him that he was asked to become Elder and asked what the Reverend thought of it. The Reverend was a really sick man at the time and got ready to go through a serious operation. He said: 'Well, you'd be just as good as any other.' So he was voted in as an Elder and he has been Elder ever since.

More people are moving out of the neighbourhood. New homes are being built. One can rent them at a low rate. Elderly people move out as well to the new home for the elderly. The houses are abandoned and immediately vandalized by young people who come in with trucks and get the carpets, the railings, the bathroom fixtures and take the windows out. So when the owner comes, it becomes too costly for him to fix up the place for living. When he does get tenants in, they don't pay the rent.

The Elders used to visit the sick and the shut-ins, in groups of two. Somehow it stopped. But there is a committee to set it up again. They are supposed to receive some pamphlets and literature. They're still in the making. When they do go out again, they can leave these little pamphlets with the people.

The Elder worked in the mines in West Virginia for about eighteen years. He came to Philadelphia in 1956 to look for work because mechanization took the work out of the miners' hands. In Philadelphia he worked as a lumber counter, as a carpenter, and as a mechanic in a car company. But then he had this bad accident. He came out of the seventh floor window. He was fixing the window and the whole thing gave way. He was supposed to become a wheelchair patient for the rest of his life, but now he seems better. Throughout the week he goes often to church. If there is some work to be done, he is called, comes down and helps in any possible way. The church is always open. They had a group that used to play sports, basketball, football; the boys had to come in and to take their equipment. They even had a pool table, a ping-pong table and many more things, but the boys destroyed the equipment. So they had to begin locking the door after a certain hour.

At one time the neighbourhood was plagued by gang wars. The Reverend called group meetings together, and all the gangs came. Soon, the gang wars stopped. By letting them come to church, meet and talk together, all the gang wars and all the killing stopped.

The church stands in the middle of the neighbourhood. People who are lonely can come. The church finds them shelter as well as blankets, clothes and food. In the summer young people and the elderly can come in for a snack. The church also takes the kids out of town in the summer.

'The part that I really like is just like sister and brother thing there, it's a certain feeling that you get that you belong to somebody. It makes you feel that after you get there that you're something special. You have any concerns? Everybody get up and speak to your little concerns and some time that you think that you got big problems then you hear somebody else's problems, your problem's nothing and that's the thing what is called congregational concerns. That is really the main part that I like the best about the church. Because any burden, any burden that you got, you got family problem, financial problem, just any problem you can get up and open your mouth freely, you don't have to be carrying that burden around with you, you can open up and let it come out.' And then I asked him, 'It is as if you have given it to Christ?' 'That's right,' he said, 'that's right and I've had quite a few, quite a few and they've been worked away through the church . . . just myself, I really appreciate it, appreciate that and every member.'

'I don't know too much about Presbyterian but here's something else, something else. Sometimes I would actually say that it don't have a denomination, there's something special, something special.'

(xiii) The Café du Monde resounds with loud laughter

'The body of Jesus is taken down from the cross.'

The Café du Monde resounds with loud laughter, a thousand and one conversations, the shouting of waiters, the jingling of glasses, cups and quarters at the cash register and the tinkling of the ah! and oh! in the mouths of children, mothers and worthy fathers of families. No conversation between the Monsignor and me is possible. We also have to allow the people around us to get used to this Roman collar in their midst.

I met him half an hour ago in a bishop's rectory. Because of the centralized structure of the Catholic church, the group of leaders that in the final analysis runs a diocese, even in a large city, is a small group of people. After some time you get to know that family of men who willingly or not accumulate the main positions in a given area. The very fact that a small group of people heads almost everything also means that if ever a clear vision were present, a strong common intuition of the priorities that are ahead, it would be possible to implement them very widely, on the condition that those perceptions are really the fruit of listening, of a discernment of what the Holy Spirit is expressing through the whole church. Unfortunately, such profound listening is not always present. It means weeping with the suffering, exposing yourself to the human agony, standing in the midst of poignant tensions, working for reconciliation with no short-cuts. If this is lacking, authority is easily perceived as callous or institutionalized, or even as oppressive, and people feel manipulated. If leaders are in the middle of the scramble, desperately trying to keep everybody together, becoming servants of reconciliation, then one day it becomes possible for them, in their turn, to spread enthusiasm, to breathe a new spirit, to awaken liveliness each time people grow discouraged once again. Going from one place to another, I wondered sometimes how many people

42

you would have to reach in the churches if you wanted to get a brilliant idea across. Two or three thousand? If those people agreed on ways of renewal, humanly speaking you would have that renewal in twenty-four hours. A telex would be enough. This is the strong side of centralized structures. To be honest, I have to add that this thought came to me in a more dismal way. I was suddenly struck by the fact that this whole generation of leaders, enablers, animators and listeners would be replaced in five or ten years and would be dead soon after, which leads to the consideration of the Church's continuity from generation to generation. Not everything will depend on this generation; although we stand on the shoulders of our forefathers, as soon as we fall down, others will stand up and lead the church a bit further on its winding pilgrimage.

The Bishop told me that Monsignor was giving a mission next door to the church and it would not surprise him if the preacher stayed in church for another hour of prayer and contemplation after the people had left. His ministry of reconciliation is nourished out of those depths. Formerly pastor at St Francis de Sales, a black parish, he had left his crowd and the certainties that go with it for a free-wheeling ministry of preaching in one parish after the other, like a pilgrim. When the Monsignor, jovial and warm, finally came out of the church, I was transplanted by a nice gesture of hospitality into the whirlwind of New Orleans' simple pleasures of coffee and beignets. He used to come here on Sunday afternoons with his parents.

He was committed to integration and equality even before his days in the seminary. His father was a businessman who owned a great deal of land and a number of houses in the city; a large housing development was named after him in the area of St Francis de Sales, around Loyola Avenue and Luther King Drive. In his family everybody was conscious of the need for better housing and for better life in public housing. The parents were also very strict in not allowing any racial undertone in the conversations. But

43

studying some sociology in the seminary, he became even more aware of the fact that blacks had been made to feel unwelcome in the church, even after the Civil War when there was supposed to be freedom. The Catholic Church had never had special churches for the blacks; there was only one church and everybody was supposed to go to the same one. The white parishioners, however, would make them feel unwelcome. In the different parishes where he worked — actually predominantly white parishes — he became more and more conscious of this persisting prejudice that gnawed at the foundations of the Church. Something had to change radically if this were to be the truly Christian and Catholic Church. He got into trouble by trying to do things, and the people would urge him to move to a black parish instead. But he never felt that way, because where change was needed was precisely in the predominantly white parishes; there the people had to be helped to change their hearts and their minds. Finally the day came when he was asked to go to St Francis, at a time in his life when he became interested in his current work of preaching parish missions in the perspective of spiritual renewal and reconciliation. He was needed in this parish. Finally after eight years he felt 'moved by the Lord' to ask again to become a free preacher. He still talks about St Francis as if he is the pastor though he is not any longer; probably the experience was so strong that it is still part of him. It must have been quite a change to move from the neighbourhood of the Magnolia Housing Project to a Motherhouse in Metairie.

New Orleans always maintained a certain closeness and mixing between whites and blacks but today whites gentrify old black neighbourhoods like the Faubourg Marigny and the lower Garden District or flee to the white suburbs, repeating a process which many American cities have gone through but which maybe could have been avoided in New Orleans because of the uniqueness of its history. The traditional geographical fragmentation of black neighbourhoods in the city is changing. Those neighbourhoods are becoming more and more isolated from the mainstream of city life as a result of the sprawling suburban developments where blacks are out of sight. But historically, there has been a conviviality between whites and blacks. Prejudices run deep but an affinity expresses itself through the capacity to inter-relate on a personal level, in a way that may sometimes seem paternalistic but that in general is rooted in a deeply shared history. One would not find this affinity so readily in other parts of the world. Here is a priest who worked eight years in a black parish and who is himself from New Orleans. What did he discover about the Christian faith by being with blacks? One thing he discovered is that under-neath the human problems we face, the basic joys, struggles, suffering, sin, successes, failures we all share, a certain response to life is characteristic of black people. The word 'soul' expresses it. Black people resonate more deeply with the joys and sorrows of life. The priest also found that in meeting with them, Catholics or Protestants or others who don't belong to any church, there always is room to talk about God, to invite them to pray and to share. He visited a small prison on a Christmas night. In that prison blacks and whites were at that time separated. On the floor where the whites were, he introduced himself and said that he wanted to read the Gospel and to pray with them. Only one man came forward while the others simply sat there. On the next floor where the blacks were, he said that he wanted to bring the good news of the birth of the Saviour, and all the men came up with open hearts, hungry for the Lord. Among the blacks are deep roots of faith. Faith kept them going during the days of slavery.

His sensitivity to the issue of segregation but even more his faith experience with the blacks have prepared him for his wandering ministry of reconciliation. He thinks that 'the church is coming alive more' and that a spiritual renewal is going on. He sees it in the coming together of blacks and whites willing to let old wounds be healed, even if there is still suspicion and deep prejudice. Reconciliation seems

45

impossible and many forces work against it but 'God can heal that'; '. . . justice and peace will come from the Lord if we open our lives to Him.' The basic reason why he has involved himself in this ministry is that, having talked about social justice and integration primarily to white congregations, he often noticed that what he said was not heard because people's hearts were not open. He feels this renewal and coming together will increase. He sees a greater social concern emerging both on the level of neighbourhoods through community action organizations and on a broader scale through the concern for peace and disarmament. He wants to help people encounter Jesus Christ and surrender to him and to his Spirit. Because only then will they be ready for the full Gospel and be able to change their attitude toward everything in life and to see their neighbours and the life of the community in a new way. He says: 'I call people to a new surrender'.

(xiv) 'God is my all and all'

'Jesus is laid in the tomb.'

I am sitting in a newly built church in a Chicago ghetto, waiting for the Archbishop's arrival. The church, replacing a huge Romanesque and Byzantine structure, is conceived as a parish centre containing a worship centre that can be divided with wooden sliding doors, a primary school, a pre-school, a parish hall and some offices. For a parish of two hundred families and as many children, it doesn't look big and the setting is simple. A banner says: 'Gateway to Heaven'. Across the aisle is a chapter of 'Gracious Ladies' with blue berets, white blouses and skirts who belong to the honour guard. Yellow stripes hang diagonally across their breasts. The men behind are knights of St Peter Claver and wear Napoleon-style hats embellished by blue, green or yellow feathers falling down on yellow chasubles. In their right hands they hold thin swords.

The theme of the dedication service, the programme says, will be 'the church where we shall always find a ladder like Jacob's, leading from earth to heaven'. Like the stairway in Jacob's dream, we are grounded in this world but our destiny reaches up to the heavens. Grounded? Or mired? This is one of the poorest neighbourhoods of the city. The policeman who drove me to the church because I looked lost walking past abandoned buildings, started the conversation with a Jeremiah-like complaint about all the problems, drugs, murders, alcohol, muggings, housing conditions, depravity. At crossings people furtively looked at me thinking that I had been mugged and that we were searching for the offender. The police car, at five minutes before the start of the ceremony, stopped right in front of the church, exactly where the men stood whose task it was to accompany the dignitaries, more glorious than I. Anyhow, I was led to the front row and offered a seat, where I tried to justify my presence to surprised neighbours.

But then the service starts; we are supposed to stand up and to join the others in climbing Jacob's ladder. The singing lifts me up. Every hymn circles around that axiom of the poor: in the depths of suffering there is a road to joy. Through singing, suffering people touch a heaven of ecstasy. A soloist who is half-black, half American–Indian comes forward and starts to sing with his eyes far beyond the assembly and his mouth as round as a smoker blowing rings in the air. It is the most beautiful hymn I have ever heard. And the echo of his singing will resound in me for a long time: 'God is my today and my tomorrow, God is my all and all . . . light in darkness, God is, he is my all and all, God is my protection, God is my all and all.'

No human suffering equals that of Christ's agony which lasts until the end of the world. In God, Christ's suffering, welcomed, offered and surrendered, becomes endless love, redemption and resurrection. Unimaginable as this may seem, we are invited to identify our suffering with Christ, to entrust the burdens of humanity at the foot of the cross and to let our agonies be transfigured into love of God and love of people. Slowly and patiently we accept that our suffering, the core of our existence, no longer belongs to ourselves, it becomes God's own (which it has always been). Whenever we are unable to abandon ourselves, Christ's own abandonment dwells in us, Christ's own suffering becomes flesh in us. Now Passion and Resurrection, the two faces of God, are rooted in us. For us as persons and as a people, finally reconciled, Christ's resurrection takes over our poor lives and leads us into the mystery of God. Then we know to whom we belong.

2

Carrying Each Other

The discovery of suffering in people's lives may awaken in us feelings of guilt and shame, of anger and rejection. As soon as we are willing to read in a contemplative way in their lives the passage of that man of Galilee who sacrificed himself out of love, we are led out of ourselves into a communion without limits. We enter into concentric circles of belonging.

A first dimension of this belonging lies in the fact that we carry one another. Any belonging starts with the recognition of this basic fact of life: no one is only himself or herself. The reality of this solidarity so very deep in ourselves has been given to us. It is there, although most of the time it is buried, concealed and forgotten. We have to let it rise again. Maybe one day we will discover that we were sanctified by the people we shared with, or even by others because of their very resemblance to the Suffering Servant. The pleading that comes from the people of the Beatitudes, in Abraham's time or today, is part of the work of redemption which Christ and his people pursue until we will have reached our destinations. We, too, have a ministry, a ministry of presence and of intercession. Why do we still feel alone sometimes in spite of this profound belonging? Courage sinks. We miss signals of progress, confirmation by visible results. How then are we to live out our vocation? Find friends, find witnesses who express in their lives what you are searching for, who make visible your own vocation. They will be the stars above you, pointing out your journey. Carried forward by them, inspired by them, you will dare again to take some steps toward Christ and become able to carry others, without needing signs and astonishing surprises.

My self is not enough

In the smoking section of the Greyhound bus two young people had been talking for a very long time in the row behind me. Although trying to sleep, I couldn't avoid hearing bits of the conversation overtopping the purring of the sleepers and the whirring of the motor. Apparently they had been sent by some kind of gospel group to a convention. Still drowsy, I couldn't at first detach my mind from some insistent thinking about the sleepless eyes of the cherubim I had read about in a hymnal. But then their voices sounded like an alarm clock.

He: 'You know, me and my friends find the church boring. To go to a movie, watch the Dodgers, go to Central Park, OK, that's nice. But church? No way. If I could do it my way, I would build up tents between churches so that people could walk from one place to another in long Sunday processions. Something you'd never seen before. Like a little zoo for the children with apes and giraffes, a place to learn Bible stories through mime and street theatre, a store for people who want to invent new clothing styles, rooms for listening conferences about problems in the community, a place for playing music and for singing. . . . At certain times a bell would ring, everybody would kneel and pray five minutes like the Muslims do when the man in the minaret starts to shout into the microphone. You know, the church doesn't have anything to offer for me.'

She: 'I'm completely different from you. Why do people think they always have to organize? You got music concerts, gags, comedians or ambassadors as preachers only in order to attract people. I think a church should be what it was meant to be, a place of prayer and community. That would be more the case, if people didn't panic about the empty pews. And if they would allow God to work in the church. There are always carnivals and attractions, but the church is a place where you can find yourself, through silence, prayer and praising God.'

He: 'But you are always so quiet. If you think like that nothing will happen. It's always been that way in the church. If the church would have the courage to begin from scratch, for example, by constructing a building with only a ceiling and an altar, or even completely underground, incredible things would happen.'

She: 'You're going to be disappointed at the convention. I hear there's nothing original. The people have simply decided that their life in the Church should be as close to the Gospel as possible. I see this as a powerful expression of simplicity and purity. An unbelievable challenge comes across. I think you will like it in the end.'

By this time I was impatient to take part in their conversation. They agreed to let me do so. I said that in history books and in newspapers one reads only about what is spectacular and often about negative developments in the Church. The young woman understands what I mean. She says that even in her own city it would be worthwhile to publish a newsletter in which members of her group would simply describe every month all the hidden signs of the Gospel they have discovered. An evening of prayer in prison where one of them played on the guitar and sang spirituals; a group of young people who met for morning prayer together with a priest before they went to school; a young woman who left the city to join a community of sisters in New Guinea for two years to work there as a nurse; young people who offer a year as volunteers in a poor area; a prayer for peace in a government building at Pentecost; a young man who goes to every anti-nuclear demonstration and has been in jail three times; a parish where fifty Asian refugees have been welcomed and supported. She says that the life of the congregations is more deeply built up and enriched by those hidden initiatives than by many exterior reforms. The young man suggests that we should bring all those people regularly together as a celebration of the People of God and discover that basically everybody already does something and that the role of the clergy and parish teams would be to reveal those gifts and acts, confirming the people, offering to assume whatever their step forward may be as a ministry that has an essential part in the ministry of the whole body. Some sharing could make all those little steps visible and could encourage those who still hesitate. I say that people are quickly discouraged if they have to confront the challenge of a maximal demand. Shouldn't we explain to them that a total commitment expresses itself less in the multiplicity of commitments than in the depth with which somebody involves himself or herself in whatever is within reach of his or her gifts?

Later, dozing off in the bus, I see in a dream the two looking at a large book laid out on a pulpit full of coloured prints. We are in a room with tall crenelated windows in an English Tudor-style mansion. Through the window I see a big spreading oak tree. The first two pages of the book have splendidly ornamented initials, the first beginning with a 'c' and the second with an 'h'. The catalogue in my hand tells me that the Benedictine monk who painted them wanted to include inside of the long curves of the initials all that had obscured the light of life in two thousand years. Maybe this was a way of exorcizing, or a homeopathic antidote. The reproduction in the catalogue shows a kind of microscopic Bosch painting with Constantine enthroned as a bishop, shelves and shelves of books surrounding Assisi's roads, black mantles and glistening swords of the Inquisition in a landscape of Scotch mist, crusaders hurling lances at people standing on ladders leaning against the walls of Acre, Servet burning in Geneva, tribunals driving people to tribulation, Dr Jekylls hiding Mr Hydes, Christians dressed up as soldiers in a tropical jungle with dead bodies all around, images of proud bourgeois coming out of church on Sunday in seventeenth century Amsterdam, Jews under pogrom persecutions in Spain, Borgias on papal thrones, blacks sitting on backless benches in the back of churches, Christians in a mass gathering acclaiming Hitler, rich buildings and villas with pious slogans written on the walls next to slums and favellas, bishops blessing an anti-ballistic missile called 'Peacekeeper', many suffering children. . . . But as I look at the reproduction, I hear the noise of scraping and scratching. The young people must have been so weary because of this evocation of a scandalizing history that they had decided to erase the pages together with the initials. But the young woman says to me: 'Don't you see that underneath the paintings another image has been printed, certainly a very long time ago? Why did the monk cover it? Please help us, because maybe there is a message in it that is very important today.' At first I had not liked the scraping. It seemed to symbolize throwing everything overboard, a lack of realism also, a refusal of human limitations. It is idealistic, I thought, to want to start things over again and again, to start from scratch after having peeled and sifted whatever does not resemble yourself.

But I must say the picture that appeared from underneath all those images of violence was beautiful. A house with red roofing in which people were breaking bread and eating a meal together, joyfully, simply. A kind of a mosque with bells in the tower toward which a bunch of people, designed as if together they formed one heart, are travelling, children jumping in the air, older people leaning on the shoulders of their sons and daughters, a black choir singing, other children held high in the air by their fathers, mothers arm in arm, handicapped persons in their wheelchairs. Nobody looks much richer than the others, but each one is wearing a different colour. Some people give away books and jewels but those who receive them give them away too. It is quite an experience to decipher such an old miniature with people lined up, each one having something in his hand up to the last one, who stands at the entrance of what must be the other end of the mosque, in an attitude of wonder. We can't see what is going on inside, but it is as if everybody in the painting, though still outside, is already within, filled with a kind of fear. But I think it is a fear full of respect, as close to love as were the calligrapher's hand and the light in the eyes of the people in his painting.

We stop along the way in a diner. The young man struggles with the question of how efficient one can be. He says that every generation tries again to renew, to reform, to remodel, to reintroduce, to reconcile, and, finally, they seem to repeat old errors and heresies. They have the impression of moving forward, but they discover in the end that there is no progress at all. For instance, churches unite their efforts in one place, but at the same time others, upset by that reconciliation, break off. What then is the meaning of our efforts? He understands that the difference between efficiency and fruitfulness is important. We are invited to bear fruit in the perpetuation of Christ's ministry, fruit that is invisible to ourselves. Our task is to be authentic and to root our lives as closely as possible in the Gospel, and then we can be confident that it has an effect, even if an invisible one: it builds something of the Kingdom of God. I tell them that in my opinion a lot of energy is liberated as soon as we are not dependent any longer on visible results, anxiously waiting for those results to prove ourselves. If, on the contrary, we build up the Church on the level of our being, not first of all through our activities and anxious reforming, then we will certainly be ready to adapt ourselves to changes that occur either by consensus or by the pressure of outer circumstances. Even if the Church, I say, is completely uncreative, inactive and apparently uninteresting, it is still the place where we have discovered many fundamental things for our lives, where we pray, sing, hear the Bible, and come to the Eucharist, and where we can assume some ministry, and find something beyond our egoisms. In the Church Christ is celebrated.

The young man recalls Stalin's question to the Pope: 'How many divisions do you have?' — meaning to say that power is something other than spiritual gatherings, humble prayers and poor people. He is worried by the fact that fewer and fewer people need the Church. They say that you can be a perfect Christian without the Church. Therefore, in many places you find only small groups of people who still believe. But the young woman does not think numbers are important. She says that being Christian is the task of living out God's love for every person. It is not getting everybody into that building we call the church, although it would be nice to see full churches once again. The Church has a much more mystical vocation, she says, because in Christ she — that is to say, we all — bear the burdens of all the other people and in offering them in prayer we make redemption concrete in our time. It is not an easier life with more philosophical clarity about the origins or the finalities of the world but a secret that becomes present in us, a secret that we are invited to whisper throughout the whole human family.

Later on, she explains that their travelling is not exceptional. Their congregation sends them out from time to time as part of a new ministry called 'listening teams'. These listening teams go to other places to pray, to listen to other people's suffering and hopes, enriching their own experience and insights. Visitors also go to other continents, especially to countries where people are oppressed or persecuted. They create 'embassies of reconciliation'. I heard about one in Namibia, another one in East Germany. They enter into these countries with the help of their specialties: some are anaesthetists or mathematicians or potters, professions that are rare. Once admitted, they live among the people with a commitment to search for reconciliation. Apparently, they don't act in a spectacular way, but they receive much inside information, allowing other people who can't travel to be aware of what is going on in the world and to feel a part of things. This is meant to be not a spiritual tourism but almost a retreat, a search for Christ among other people. To prepare themselves they focus on John 15: 'I am the true vine.' Here are some questions they shared with me: What does it mean for my life that I am a branch from the vine of Jesus Christ, that my life is grounded in his life? If it is God who tends my life, why has God guided my growth to this time and place? What are the diversions and distractions in my life which bear no fruit, which might just as easily be cut away? What areas of my life need pruning, sharper focusing, greater attention so that they may be strengthened, and so strengthen me? What is the word or phrase or image which clears my vision so I can remember who I was born to be? To what matters might I attend so that I would be more free to dwell in Christ and Christ would be more able to shine within me and through me? What are the fruits God wants me to bear so that his will may be done?

With all this sharing our conversation becomes more personal during the last miles of the bus ride. The sun is setting, stillness becomes our light. I want to explain to them that for me belonging means, first of all, to acknowledge that I do not exist by myself and for myself. A first belonging precedes my personal choices, desires, achievements. If the Church is composed of many concentric circles, the innermost circle is a communion of people who belong to one another because they have given up their own lives into Christ's hands. They don't own themselves any more. It is a sign of growth in the spiritual dimension if you are not ready to take decisions in your own life without including the others in your own decision-making. You are a prisoner of Christ's communion and led out of the prison of your exclusive self. No one is only himself or herself. Individualism is dead, although it re-emerges all the time and has to be transformed into belonging. To be a Christian is to renounce our own wishes which would project ourselves on the forefront of our existence. At the same time, this very renunciation announces the birth of the other in us. In so far as we are able to diminish our own claims, there will be room for others. Others will not appear as an additional issue to deal with after having affirmed one's own existence. Others are part of yourself. You look into the world simultaneously with your own eyes and with those of others. You are married to humanity. You don't find a justification for your own existence in your own happiness or success or well-being because you exist with and through others. The essence of church belonging is this carrying each other very deep inside oneself. A beautiful story, which I read once in one of Charles Williams' books, summarizes this common belonging grounded in our belonging to Christ, so I retell it to the two young people just before we arrive at our destination. The story itself could be called 'Destination'.

Prince Emmanuel gives a party. Everyone receives an invitation. One specific instruction: masquerade ball. Clothe yourself with the attributes of the other. The invitations are distributed all over the city. One arrives at the home of a man of quality. Nothing, neither affairs nor intrigues, hinders this man in honouring, from time to time, the princely throne. 'Why', he says to himself, 'I know the prince very well, I have travelled in his cars. He will understand that I remain faithful to my motto "*Egomet semper*", "Always myself".' The evening arrives and the party approaches. A servant stops him from entering: 'Sir, this party demands that you scrupulously observe the invitation. Before bowing before the throne, we need virtues, beauty, and the gifts of others.' He allows the man to have a glimpse of the party through the open door. Everywhere in the big ballroom and on the staircases he sees the splendour of exchange. One person wears the courage of his brother, another the energy of his wife, while she, further away in the crowd, radiates the constant patience of her husband. Elsewhere a young fiancé has clothed himself with the openness and goodness of the young woman he loves. A father wears the success of his son, and the son is not ashamed to wear the wisdom of his father. Now he understood that no one is only himself or herself.

Pleading for a guilty city
I learned to read at four by deciphering the stories about Abraham in the Bible. The Bible nourished me as much as potatoes nourish one in wartime. At four I heard Abraham pleading for Sodom: 'Please, don't be angry, Lord, and I

57

will speak just once more. What if only ten are to be found?"
So very early I understood a little bit that solidarity with
others can express itself also through intercession, and that
the intercession especially of those who suffer is heard by
God. The poor, the persecuted, those who mourn, the
humble, the pure of heart have a voice and are heard. In intercession we lay before God whatever weighs us down, in
ourselves and in others. But the poor and those who suffer,
when they address themselves to God, lay down their whole
existence, their very existence is intercession, a cry for help
and understanding. They are closer to Christ than anybody
else because they have no security to rest on other than the
evidence of their utter dependence. The poor feel a link with
God. No mental exercises, no long meditations, no need for
retreat houses, no need for concentration using some left-
over time. They bear in themselves the glorious opening
that leads into heaven like Jacob's ladder. Through God
their suffering becomes a pleading for an unjust world. And
although they are still en route, always fighting against
death, never fully resurrected, always striving to be new-
born, God listens to them. I want to belong to that people of
the beatitudes.

Last year in New Orleans, I heard the story of a turn-of-
the-century black washerwoman told by her grandson, himself an old man. I was again struck by the way the poor are
able to carry before God those who oppress them and to
contribute in Christ to the salvation of humanity. The
grandson told me that a while back a state-wide senior citizens Mass was held at St Louis Cathedral for the first time.
Senior citizens came from all over Louisiana by bus and
train and car. The cathedral was overflowing. The Archbishop was present. Throughout the history of the Church
in New Orleans, never had a black lay person been invited
to come up to the altar to do one of the readings, the two im-
pediments being colour and clergy prerogative. Historically, colour has been the deepest division, the Church
contradicting itself and denying its universality. Even now

the map of the archdiocese on which the parishes are outlined show red and green boundaries, red indicating the white parishes, green the black ones. The boundaries overlap. This means that in the structure of the archdiocese and in the outline of the boundaries of the parishes a certain segregation has been maintained. But now this old black man walked down the cathedral aisle to the altar. The first time a black *priest* celebrated Mass at the cathedral was in 1938, on the occasion of the eighth National Eucharistic Congress that met in the city of New Orleans with Cardinal Mundelein from Chicago as papal legate. The same black layman was present. He belonged to a committee of the congress which was planning a meeting for business and professional men and women. He fought the proposal to have the whites gather at Loyola and the blacks at Xavier University. He lost. The only concession that he obtained was that the two meetings would not be held simultaneously but one after the other. The official reason for this separation had been that there was no place big enough to gather both groups together. He also fought the proposal to reserve the ground floor for the whites and the first floor for the blacks at the closing session in an auditorium, and he won that. He thought it was time for the Church to take a stand, to break through the divisions.

At the beginning of the century, the grandmother of the black layman still had to sit in the balcony among the ladies of Christian Doctrine (Les Dames et Demoiselles de la Doctrine Chrétienne). Although blacks were Catholic, they were not permitted to sit in the churches but were relegated to the back or, like in the cathedral, to the loft. Up in the balcony a handful of blacks, the servants of the wealthy, gathered together. When the wealthy people came to the cathedral, they brought along their servants, because after Mass they walked over to the French market to buy provisions for dinner (there were no refrigerators then). The slaves carried the market basket. The mistresses of the house would pick out the vegetables. Although slavery was legally abolished in 1865, the system was perpetuated in many ways. In other churches the blacks sat on three wooden benches in the back. All around the area of St Augustine, rich people had their homes. The grandmother of the black layman went to that church because she worked as a washerwoman on Esplanade Avenue. She was a profoundly religious woman. Every night she used to pray with her family, after 9 p.m., the rosary and the litany to the Blessed Virgin, in French. She prepared herself a whole year long to receive communion at Easter time. She always had kept her first communion clothes, in memory of the first time she had received the Lord. She kept them in the closet in a box wrapped in silk paper. Every Easter she would clothe herself with some part of them. And at the end of her journey this dress, the shoes and everything that was in the box accompanied her to the grave.

This black lady never wanted to sit on the benches in the back of *l'église de Saint Augustin*; she chose to sit on the steps of the large confessional box. Her grandson did not understand this and asked his grandmother why. She sat there, she said, in order to pray for the people who were sitting in the seats because she felt compassion for those people who segregated her. Walking across Rampart Street to St Augustine's, walking on the pavement where she walked, I have often thought about this woman pleading for a guilty city. A very traditional piety has often allowed people, on the basis of what might seem a routine, on the basis of obligations, regularity and a host of traditions, to give birth to holiness.

At that time, humiliation existed in the most insidious ways. Shopping in the big stores on Canal Street, few people could pay cash. If you bought something for a hundred dollars, you would pay ten dollars down and two dollars each week. If the bill was addressed to a white man, it would be written to Mister so and so. If the bill came to a black man, only the first name and family name would be mentioned. When the Sisters of Charity began to let black nurses practise at Charity Hospital, the white nurse would be addressed as Miss so and so, the black nurse as Nurse so and so. The Board of Education would call a black teacher by her first name, and her colleagues would call her by her family name. Fifty years ago, these little things were there to increase the idea of inferiority. But a black washerwoman pleaded for a guilty city.

In every black family, a few generations back, one could find completely white members of that same black family. Intermingling between the white plantation owners and the slaves ('I was a slave to white labour, I was a slave to white lust . . .') was frequent. Even today you don't know if the person who sits next to you is white or black. Black mothers of white complexion eighteen or nineteen years old, who couldn't find work, left home and found work as whites. That was an accepted thing. Sometimes they would visit their family late at night. Light-skinned people in the black families had this advantage. The others couldn't do anything else but sweep floors or take other subordinate jobs. The intermingling, with the white in the predominant role, must have created an imaginary thread that bound blacks and whites together somehow. Is that the reason why in New Orleans there has never been a revolt? In 1910 a black man, Robert Charles, stood up and refused to remain behind the screen in the streetcar, asking for recognition as a man. In the sixties there were only minor insurrections. A black washerwoman pleaded for a guilty city.

Someone wrote me recently that I shouldn't think too much about the theme of suffering in New Orleans' history because so much good had been done for the blacks. And it is true that the Church has never been monolithic like a political party or a racial organization could be. The Capuchins certainly had a subtle way of alleviating some of the ills of slavery. Père Antoine lived in his hut behind St Louis Cathedral, helping everybody alike. The Capuchins were not in open conflict with the established government, but they worked on the slave owners in order to awaken in

61

them a kinder disposition to their slaves. They visited the plantations outside the city limits and baptized fifty slaves at a time. Because the masters were baptized they hoped to bring about some improvement in the slaves' conditions by baptizing them as well. In the archives of St Louis Cathedral one finds the huge books with the baptism records, handwritten by the Capuchin Fathers, mentioning that they had visited the plantation of Monsieur so and so and baptized slaves. They added a line of description of the skin colour, black, very black, very fair, light, black-brown. The names of the infants were put down with the approximate age, the sex and the height. Compassion is also part of New Orleans' church history. But at the same time blacks were admitted in no hospitals except Charity Hospital, and there only at the back entrance, where the Sisters took care first of the whites and followed the law of separation of the races until 1960. But a black washerwoman pleaded for a guilty city.

This washerwoman was born in Louisiana on a plantation owned by French people. She spoke French before she learned English. All the prayers the grandson learned were in French. The grandmother was the matriarch of the house and the grandchildren had to go to her, kneel down, say the prayer to '*Ti Jésus*' and learn the catechism. They didn't live on the premises in the one-family homes on Esplanade Avenue but went there to work, the grandfather as cook, the grandmother as washerwoman, the mother as maid. The grandson didn't think he was poor, although he was very poor according to today's standards. He thought he was a very wealthy boy. He had one blue suit which he wore on Sundays and holidays, some pants and shirts that each day were immaculately clean, and he went to school. He had no need for money because he could walk to school and back. But his whole family sacrificed to make it possible for his sister and him to go to school. For one year he went to a very fashionable school for black boys of the so-called better families run by a black man who had been educated in

France and Spain. His grandmother could neither write nor read. But she taught all the stories of the operas to her grandson; she knew everything about Chopin. She made up little prayers in French for her grandson. At home they had a piano, a mandolin and a guitar and he learned in his youth all the French nursery rhymes, like 'Sur le pont d'Avignon'. Going to school was not only a privilege; it was an honour. Many of the people the grandson grew up with wanted their children to go to school, but the financial drain was such that many boys started to work after having finished the eighth grade. In the household in which he grew up — with his mother, grandmother and two aunts — there was nothing, absolutely nothing as important as to go to church and to school. You had to learn. Growing up in that kind of environment, children later became doctors and teachers.

Leaving St Augustine's church, crossing Rampart Street, I find the silence reigning in the quarter on this evening during Advent. People's steps on the narrow sidewalks echo against the stucco walls and the wrought iron ornaments on flowered balconies. The patios, crammed with magnolias, radiate in the interior courtyards. Something ghostly haunts places where history has outlived itself and boundless suffering accumulated through the ages has flooded the artificial levees of people's way of life. And a trumpet in the distance chants the lament of the old ceaseless sacrifices. A little bell rings for evening prayer. How good it is to have created another silence on the border of the quarter, a silence lifted up by the Advent music that lights upon whoever enters the one-story-high Tau House. The floor-length windows are closed off by shutters that only let the most audacious sunbeams enter, illuminating one face after another at the table where out of thick brown paper we are cutting the words of the Beatitudes, words to be hung with the angels' hair on the Christmas tree. The partition around the fireplace between two rooms has been taken away. Two communicating spaces are thus created, one for the Word,

63

one for the Eucharist, and during the time of prayer we move around and around from one to the other like on a merry-go-round. Under the high ceiling the incense ascends. I feel as if I am in an Eastern Orthodox hermitage on a mountaintop facing mirrors, icons and images of Christ surrounded by a forest of candles twinkling and winking in the falling darkness. A tenor and a bass strike up the litanies of Advent, and I join in the prayer of the poor who plead for the world: 'O King of the Nations . . . Cornerstone, you make opposing nations one; come and save us. You formed us all from the clay . . . O Morning Star, Splendour of light eternal and bright Sun of Justice, come and enlighten all who live in darkness and in the shadow of death.'

Finding friends who stand on the horizon
We enter into a hidden communion with people by taking up the challenge we are called to live out as our vocation. A vocation, however personal, does not set us apart or keep us aloof but leads us into a wider communion and reveals this communion. We are becoming part of a living mosaic. We are woven into a fabric made up of invisible threads. Once my thread will have hurtled through the meshes, the harmony of my tone will be blending with all the others. There is room for all in the fabric. Everyone's streak contributes to the beauty of the whole design. Everybody can bring his or her own colours into the fabric which is gradually being woven until its completion. But how can one make sense out of this hidden solidarity in settings that almost systematically foster anonymity and isolation exacerbated by overcrowding and barrenness? Should one become a hermit in order to understand what communion is all about? But most people live in areas that look like a forest of towers, an assembly line of obelisks or an endless number of matchboxes thrown together in a desert wilderness. They don't even have a neighbourhood. What is called 'neighbourhood' represents the complete opposite of whatever may have been envisaged as settlement, hamlet, village or city: a

parched landscape of abstract parallels leaving just enough space for the wind to blow through. Any architecturally designed space for intimacy or togetherness is left out. How then to believe that our life has been welcomed into a wider communion, that our life bears fruit in invisible ways and that the existence of other people is at the origin of our own blossoming desert?

We need friends. We need to know some people in whom we recognize our own vocation. Find friends and witnesses who stand on your horizon. Make a list of people you admire. Look up in your address book the names of people you have met who conveyed to you, just recently, some dynamism, some perspective. To think of them is today your first responsibility. These people, all over the world, who stand under the arch of a rainbow, for you — that is right now your first church. It is your first circle of friends who reveal to you where you belong. How many do you know? Twelve? One hundred and forty-four? With whom did you feel this year an inner consonance? In whom did you recognize so much that your own vocation came again to life? You started to hope again. It is possible, it is possible, you said. They are a sign of the Gospel in your life. They carry you.

A vow of belonging

I remember a young couple in Texas, on Chihuahua Street, sitting in their lavender-coloured house (close by I saw a light green one). They seemed convinced about their long-term commitment, full of joy, rays of the sun for whoever needs their presence. They were involved in several justice and peace organizations, but what impressed me more than anything else was the peaceful way they live out their daily life as a family and as neighbours, in a real slum area. In an area of ten blocks there are ten thousand school-age children and more drugs available than in any other twenty square miles of Texas. They have been there since 1969. Many things they wanted at the outset 'to learn from the poor' have been ingrained in them. Sometimes they are reminded of what they have learned and integrated into their lifestyle by someone who comes to spend a day. The extreme generosity of the people in the *barrio*, the eagerness to help: 'If I was pregnant with my fifth child and my husband had just left me and I lived in white middle-class suburbia, away from my family, I would not know to whom to turn. But here half a dozen neighbours would say: I'll take care of your children when you go to the hospital.' They think this neighbourly helpfulness stems from the struggle for basic survival. When they go back to suburbia — as singers they have occasionally given folk music concerts at colleges as well as on the downtown riverwalk — they feel like foreigners. When they come home, they are again in touch with reality, in touch also with a place where the Gospel lives and where it is growing. In the Midwest, where they came from, they had been impressed as students by an Irish immigrant who worked with the poor and later was deported because of his involvement in draft issues. He didn't have any massive programmes but was just reaching out to the people around him. So the idea grew in them to do the same thing, to live and to share with people without large, functional programmes, to be neighbours, to help one person after another as well as to be helped by them.

In their conversation I heard coming back one expression that reveals a key option in their existence: *to see Christ in others*, to welcome neighbours with openness, at any time of the day or night, discovering how much their neighbours live a reflection of Christ, without masks, without worrying about their image. At the start they were afraid about moving from a middle-class world into a poor neighbourhood of drugs and gangs, densely populated and considered to be the roughest in the whole town. But quickly they realized that it is the same thing in the other parts of town, the only difference being that there one doesn't see it. One sees only the walls around the estates and the guards in front of them. Other kinds of crime are committed by not sharing what one could or by causing unemployment. They say that the suffering in their neighbourhood exists because of what is going on in the rich parts of town. If too much electricity is used on the North Side, people pay, but in this neighbourhood the electricity is turned off because the people can't afford to pay. As a matter of fact they no longer like the term 'poor', which implies that they are lacking something. They have only economic needs, but other things are much more important and those things can be found here. They don't want to run a programme but just to be people who share. From time to time they make a list of all their commitments and choose: work at the clinic Amistad, teaching in an elementary neighbourhood school, pulling a rickshaw as fundraising for an outdoor swimming pool for the kids of the neighbourhood, getting certification by attending classes at night, organizing a festival to raise money for the Inner City development project, setting up recreation for the kids of the area and a food and clothing pantry, taking part in the Fellowship of Reconciliation, leading a choir at Our Lady of Guadalupe. They take time for family growth and sharing.

How fulfilled life is when it is given away, gratuitously! I see him pulling the rickshaw for children who are not his own. I hear her sing 'On Our Journey', a *pasionaria* for justice and a nun in prayer rolled together. This radiant couple on Chihuahua Street have nothing but their eyes to fête me. A sprightly sparkle enlivens the singsong of our shared stories. I know its source. They remind me of one of my lifetime commitments: always to see Christ himself in my brothers.

A community on pilgrimage
Then this year I met that little gospel family of Saint Francis in Chicago. Coming from O'Hare, Uptown looked like a dumping place. As a matter of fact, the first thing people tell me is that since the Second World War it has been a dumping place for all newcomers, for poor whites

from Appalachia, for Cubans, Puerto Ricans and Mexicans, for American Indians, for Vietnamese, Laotian and Cambodian refugees and for many others. At one time it was called the Hollywood of Chicago because of the movies that were produced here. The architecture of the houses indicates that it used to be a very wealthy neighbourhood. Now, the only rich people left live on the lake front.

The Franciscans, as part of their gospel life style, make a 'pilgrimage' every Friday, 'a walk with the Lord' through the neighbourhood, simply praying for the people they meet or see. The evening before, explaining this to me, they read at the kitchen table parts of Psalm 84: '. . . Happy the people whose strength you are. Their hearts are set upon the pilgrimage. When they pass through the valley of the trees, they make a spring of it; the early rain clothes it with generous growth. They go from strength to strength . . .' So on a Friday morning I walk with one of them who is part of the Franciscan Volunteer Community. He is a young man with a very long, nonchalantly maintained beard who is the kind of person one vaguely remembers from some Russian novel, a staretz in a nutshell, an Aliosha of the derelicts, living on nothing and continuously busy with prayers and a thousand little details all for the poor. He himself looks like a transient and, as a matter of fact, has no stable home but the shelters he tries to keep open in spite of the opposition of building inspectors, neighbourhood organizations and . . . churches. He shows me his world, which is made up of underground networks of people who seem to hand out glasses of water in an ocean of misery. At first I feel as if I have to make the town crier's round.

A deep renewal has been going on among Franciscans around the world. St Francis is universally perceived as a figure who speaks very directly and powerfully to modern Christians. In my youth people called him the first Protestant saint, and I devoured the fine biographies Protestant writers had dedicated to his memory. Later, in the young adult culture of the sixties and seventies, he became the patron of all those who refused capitalism — Francis' renunciation of his father's patrimony! — and of those who advocated a return to unspoiled nature and the love of animals. These are reasons enough for Franciscans in cloistered monasteries and big study houses in suburbs, where never a poor person has set foot, to rediscover their founder. In 1968, the minister general issued an encyclical letter to the Franciscan family asking three probing questions: What are we doing in a socially beneficial way with land that we are not actually using? What are we doing to help the economically deprived? Have we initiated new forms of Franciscan life? Four Franciscans from the Chicago area were allowed to experiment with living in community. At the end of the sixties, they started by living for a month with some Brothers of Taizé on Locust Street (the neighbourhood has drastically changed, there is no Locust Street any more) on the edge of Cabrini Green, accomplishing together a ministry of presence and friendship among blacks and whites. The Taizé 'fraternities' are provisional, and as pilgrims after some time we always head elsewhere. After a few years in Chicago the brothers moved on. But the four Franciscans continued.

There were other inspirations. One of the Franciscans — who is Polish — at that time discovered the Charismatic movement. The spontaneous character of their prayer impressed him. Since then he has been going to a prayer meeting every week, first at Immaculate Conception, later at St Teresa's and even in Uptown. Franciscan Friars as well as a Sister from the convent at St Mary's have started prayer groups in the six or seven Uptown halfway houses for psychiatric patients released from mental institutions. The Uptown Baptist church is doing the same; on Saturday night they bus in the mentally handicapped for an evening of song and praise, with worship and refreshments. Many mentally retarded persons live in Uptown. They stop people on the street and ask them for a dime. No neighbourhood wants them. Uptown has become a dumping place for them.

Another important moment for the four Franciscans in their beginnings as a new community was the meeting with a couple living along the lines of the Catholic Worker movement. Together with them they moved into a building on West Armitage, renting the second and the third floors. Those houses have on each floor a kind of 'portiuncula', a round cornered room overhanging the street. One of those became the chapel. There were three distinctive things about their lifestyle, all three diverging completely from their large 'monastic' existence in the suburbs. First, they lived in a neighbourhood of the poor, mostly Puerto Rican families. Second, they took the risk of living on a welfare budget, without trying by whatever means to accumulate capital. Third, they offered hospitality to anyone who knocked on the door. One of the Franciscans, speaking of St Francis as well as of their own humble initiative, uses the expression 'kenotic'. The new style, which is also the one Francis practised, is a return to the kenotic tradition of the Church. '*Kenosis*' is the Greek word used in Philippians 2 where St Paul speaks about Christ's descent into lowliness. The kenotic tradition, the tradition of servanthood, of protest against the world and worldliness, the tradition of powerlessness, of a Church on pilgrimage, was abandoned with Constantine and the amalgamation of Church and Empire. In the late sixties many religious orders began to search in this direction. Suddenly, many felt alienated by their life in large convents and wanted to become part of a neighbourhood on a day-to-day basis, simply living among the people, even unrecognized, working like everybody else, with all the normal problems of a household, a budget, of daily responsibilities in a small group. Small groups, however, have sometimes created new tensions within the congregations. Large convents have decided to split up in small groups inside the convent, or in houses close by. After their self-imposed exile, many religious rediscovered the positive aspects of a larger community, recognizable as a sign of the Church, as a place of wider hospitality and above all, as a place of worship and liturgy, the basic witness of any religious community. Throughout the years an interpenetration has taken place between the small groups, often made up of younger religious, and the old convents that became headquarters and infirmaries.

The Franciscans have now lived on Gordon Terrace in Uptown for eight years, and because of the redevelopment and gentrification going on next door, they are considering moving again. In their house on Gordon Terrace I spent most of the time with them in the kitchen. One Franciscan comes back from a day of looking for old newspapers in the alleys. If he hears about a job, he suggests it to some Oriental family in need. The grocery stores give him surplus food for the poor. Some young people live in the house with the Fathers. Every evening while I was there some drunken man would enter, falling down on a kitchen chair and mumbling his need for help. On Wednesdays the whole gospel family comes together — the Gordon Terrace and the Sunnyside communities, third order members, a Sister, some mentally handicapped people and young people — for Mass, for sharing, for listening to a talk and for much warm laughter. A woman who belonged to the family has left recently to live as a third order member in an abandoned house in the valley around Spencer, West Virginia. There she built some hermitages in the wilderness. Also, a couple has gone to New Mexico to live in an adobe house.

At the end of our Friday pilgrimage, the Franciscan volunteer asks — begs, I should say — for my prayers and disappears on the way to some other business different from that of the surrounding business world, in the 'foolishness' of his search for God who, he knows, walks with the poor and the destitute. After the first shock of coming into the Uptown area, I feel at home now when I return to read psalms at the kitchen table, morning and evening, with a gospel family.

Since then, I often think of my Chicagoan Aliosha. He is still praying in the streets of that city, somewhere between the skidrow on West Madison and rich Park Ridge, on his

71

business tours for the poor, like the Russian pilgrim praying without ceasing: Lord, have mercy upon us, like those 'fools for Christ' we are supposed to be in the midst of a society made up of rectilinear rules and compulsive conformity. My community at the kitchen table is a little remnant of Israel, waiting for Christ to come, waiting for him among the other poor.

A life for reconciliation
In the room are representatives of a coalition of parishes on the West Side of San Antonio. The archbishop's participation in the meeting is nothing out of the ordinary; the others consider him a co-worker. The archbishop is asking the parish representatives to help Our Lady of Guadalupe, situated in the poorest section of the West Side, to become a centre for pilgrimages. He believes in pilgrimages. Ten years ago, while still a new bishop, he began an annual diocesan pilgrimage of two or three days to Our Lady of Guadalupe in Mexico City. In part, this pilgrimage is aimed at making Mexican Americans aware of their cultural roots.

He faced many obstacles in becoming a priest. At that time (he celebrated the twenty-fifth anniversary of his ordination in 1981), the Church wasn't looking for Mexican American seminarians. There was no stated policy, but all such vocations were discouraged unless the applicants had sufficient educational background. Patricio Flores had to overcome obstacles to enter the seminary. A Divine Providence sister who had founded a Mexican American congregation outside her own group composed of white, university-educated women, took the young Patricio to the bishop of Galveston-Houston. Son of a migrant and himself a migrant, Patricio was allowed to enter a Catholic high school and, later, the seminary.

Patricio's father was also opposed to the idea of his son's vocation. He went so far as to send the young man off to a Mexican border town with some money in his pocket in order to distract him with the pleasures for which the town was renowned. The young man went but the experience didn't make him waver from his aim of remaining in the seminary. Many years later, when his widowed father was living with him in a rectory in Houston, the son suggested that his father drive over to the same border town in order to have some company. His father took him up on the idea. In the border town he met the woman who would become his second wife.

Before entering the seminary, Patricio worked with his brothers and sisters in the cottonfields along what is known as the migrant trail in West Texas. One day they learned that their father, whom they had left at home ill in bed, had taken a turn for the worse. They left their fields and headed straight for home. All through the night they drove along the straight Texas roads, arriving at dawn in the town of Rosenberg, near Houston. There they stopped at a restaurant to get gas, to wash up a bit and have some breakfast. All the children except Patricio had light coloured skin. Their orders were taken, but Patricio was told that Mexicans weren't served there. Hurt, they all left the restaurant and continued on to Houston to see their father. Years later, just after Patricio was ordained a priest, the Rosenberg Knights of Columbus invited him to speak at their regular meeting. When the meeting was over, all of the assembled convened to a restaurant, as was their custom, for dinner. They had not told the young priest where they were going, but he recognized the interior of the restaurant. He was looking around when a man came up from behind and said: 'Father, this is the restaurant in which you were refused service when you stopped with your brothers and sisters. It was run by my father then, and now I have taken it over. We have tried since then to change the rules.' He was now acceptable to them because he was a priest, but there was still a long way to go before Mexican Americans would be able to take full part in Texas society, and even in the Church.

73

An artist on the West Side told me that as a child she was first of all a problem for the teachers because she had to be taught a new language. At home neither of her parents, working as hired hands on a farm first in Wisconsin then in Texas, could speak English. Each time she spoke Spanish in school, she was spanked. The teacher hit her on the back of her legs with a yardstick every time she used a Spanish word. When she was ten, she had to write on the blackboard a hundred times that she would not speak Spanish. Even to this day, her tongue gets stiff every time she speaks Spanish. The students got to the point where they wanted to speak English without an accent. Some whose name sounded Italian let people think they were Italian because they were so ashamed to be Mexican. The Catholic schools taken over by the Irish from the French (who had started them after the Mexican American War) taught the young Mexican American people how to be good Irish Catholics. They were taught to cut themselves off from their humiliated race. A kid whose grandmother was Indian would keep affirming she was a Spaniard. In the public schools it was worse. Discrimination led to the situation that there were only a very few Mexican American children making it even to junior high school. They dropped out even in 3rd, 4th or 5th grade. There were three school systems, one for the Anglos, one for the Blacks, one for the Mexicans. Even the cemeteries were divided. In a larger town, the three population groups each had a cemetery. In small towns, the cemetery was made of different sections, for white, black and Mexican.

Even today, the young people, in general, prefer to be considered as full Americans. In spite of the *paseo* on Friday evening along the main street in the small towns of Texas or the ceremony of the *quinceañera* for young girls who reach the age of fifteen, their membership in mariachi-groups and the rest of their cultural heritage, they don't speak Spanish, or do so badly, and feel humiliated if an Anglo speaks to them in Spanish. For young people to be proud of being Mexican

74

American takes a certain cultural-political awareness. The reason is that, although a certain number of Mexican Americans have climbed the social ladder, the name Mexican American is still associated with poverty, illegal crossing of the border, seasonal farmworkers, Texmex and a ritualistic Catholicism they don't always feel comfortable with. Many young people not only don't know their own history, but they refuse it as well. This in itself, in spite of all the frenetic searching for roots that kept Americans busy in their free time some years ago, is a sign of assimilation into American society, which fundamentally has always been a society with a repressed past, a society of people who decided to start on this land from scratch, a nation of creators of a new life. Until recently, Mexican Americans were pushed, not only in the wider society, but also at church or in school, to behave like Americans. In high school they were taught how to be more Anglo.

The Mexican American Cultural Center in San Antonio, where a new pastoral approach is taught for the Hispanic ministry in the Catholic Church, is the crucible of whatever is left of the Chicano movement of the late sixties. What do they teach? A lot of Mexican American history, sociology, anthropology. And, of course, Scripture, but seen in the context of discrimination, the oppression and the discovery of the cultural specificity which is the reality of the Mexican Americans. Renowned theologians and philosophers from Latin America — Gustavo Gutierrez, Leonardo Boff, Enrique Dussel — sojourn to MACC every year. They explain that God is *maestro*, which means teacher. God is teacher; we are students. God is Father and we are all brothers and sisters. If we say that God is owner, we are all co-owners; nothing belongs to us or everything belongs to us. With such a premise the message becomes to treat everyone else as equals and to feel yourself equal to them. Words like equality, fraternity, justice, so often used in the US, had no significance for Mexican Americans in the past. But as these words are put together with church and faith, they become a living reality for them. They explain that Christ came from a border area in Palestine (Galilee was a frontier). Because of this he probably spoke a mixture of languages. Mexican American Texmex is also a fruit of people living in a border area. It is not a new language, but a way of speaking English and Spanish, completing the sentence started in English by a Spanish ending and vice versa. And the borderland was poor. Mexican Americans were for a long time the poorest people in the United States. People say: what good can come from Galilee? What good are those people from Mexico? Mexican Americans have struggled in this country; they are a conquered people and they were treated as second-class people for a long time although long before the Mayflower the Mexicans were present in what later became the territory of the United States. Today, the undocumented still have to go through the same struggle. When they open the Bible, Mexican Americans bring in this whole reality of their history. As exegesis or theology, it is very far from European speculative thinking. But are these thinkers so sure to read the Bible in the right perspective from behind their thick glasses and the peaceful walls of their study? And was the Bible written for anyone else but those who have to go through oppression and persecution?

Flores became auxiliary bishop in 1970 when he was forty years old. He was the first Mexican American bishop ever consecrated. During one of his trips to administer confirmation and to give talks in the far reaches of the archdiocese, he was driving his car from Del Rio to Eagle Pass along the Rio Grande. There was no direct road between the two cities, so he had to drive fifty miles out of his way in order to reach the only road which passed through the desert. It was a cold and rainy night. Suddenly, he thought he saw a human form in the uncertain glare of his headlights. The bishop thought to himself that it was probably an animal. He continued to drive through the night, repressing the desire to know more. It was too risky to stop in the middle of nowhere at 11 p.m. But a minute later, he reproached himself, and he turned back along the road. He shouted: 'Is there anyone here? . . . Can I help you? . . . Say something. . . .' There was no response. He tried again: 'I am a priest. If I can help you, say something . . .' No answer. Finally, he shouted: 'I am Bishop Flores, tell me if I can help you'. He heard a voice, and a man stepped out of the darkness. He had entered Texas illegally. He had crossed the river at one of those places where it is possible to do so, hopping from rock to rock without even getting his feet wet. The bishop loaned the man his shirt while the car's heater dried out the one he had been wearing. They drove on to the next town to get something to eat. However, when they got there, they saw a police car. So the bishop went into the restaurant alone to get something to take out and then brought the man a bus ticket to San Antonio where he was headed in order to visit his sister, who had been hospitalized. He waited there until the man was safely on the bus.

From the time of his nomination as bishop, Flores' name came to be known far and wide among the people. He soon became a symbol of trust and security. At a time when authorities are being called into question and forced to give up pieces of their power, it is interesting to note that as soon as bishops relate the message of the Gospel to the people and the poor, when they come out of the ranks of the poor and remain faithful to their roots, they are listened to and loved. He knows what poverty is: 'To be poor is to be powerless, to experience alienation and abandonment. To be poor is to experience most sharply the lack of community caused by a breakdown of relationships. To be poor is to feel a sense of helplessness and a lack of hope. To be poor is to have little control over one's life. To be poor is to have very limited options available for responding to needs. Finally, to be poor is to be voiceless.'

Some time ago a murder of a young Salvadorian took place in Immaculate Conception parish. The general assumption was that he was killed by a neighbourhood gang. This act of violence was the result of a number of incidents between Mexican Americans and Salvadorians who had illegally entered the country and were blamed for taking work away from those who were already here. The incidents had been symbols of the violence which runs through all the neighbourhoods and people of the city, not only on the West Side where the killing happened. The archbishop was asked to be present at the funeral. The event affected him deeply since he had spent many years at Immaculate Conception. In his homily he admitted that he had been tempted to excuse himself from the service because of another commitment. In order to describe his hesitations, he used a very strong Spanish word, 'cobarde'. 'I was a coward about responding to come to this Mass,' he said with tears in his eyes, 'and to speak out to tell you that all together we must face up to these violent eruptions and also to the cowardice which tempts us to run away'.

At St Stephen's on the West Side I attend a meeting to prepare for the triduum of the Festival Guadalupeño on 12 December. Women are in charge of the preparation. At a certain moment they look at a film about the apparition of Our Lady of Guadalupe that will be shown at the festival. The only one they found has an English text, but the women think this will be even better for the young people who are more fluent in English and who don't know their traditions. The story of the apparition is not only important because of the veneration of Mary but also as a cultural symbol. Our Lady of Guadalupe is present everywhere in the churches, in the homes, on the banners of Cesar Chavez' demonstrations among the Mexicans in California. The bishop of San Diego even wears the image almost life-size on his chasuble and, reduced, on his mitre, which historically seems to be a false appropriation (the image of the Blessed Virgin the Indian called Juan Diego had seen on the hill of Tepeyac in Mexico appeared on his *tilma*, not on the bishop's!). It is an old story from December 1531. The Indian man, symbol of the poor, hears heavenly music on the hill on his way to Mass, a sign of divine communication. Our Lady appears and tells him in Nahuatl, the language of the conquered, to go to see the bishop of Mexico who is from Spain (in 1521 Cortez' conquest was completed) and to let him know that she wants a temple built in the *barriada* in the valley. In the pre-Columbian culture, a temple represented new life, the expression of a new civilization. Juan Diego was not able to convince the bishop of Mexico, a Franciscan who asked for a sign. Our Lady instructed Juan Diego to gather roses on the top of the hill, and he placed them in his cloak. In Aztec culture, flowers were even more than music, a sign of life given by the invisible God. The bishop saw the roses tumbling down in front of him and the image of the Virgin appearing in Juan Diego's cloak. And a shrine was then erected. A new meaning was given to the conquered existence of the Indians. The Virgin's image is Indian; the blue–green of the mantle, the red dress, the stars, the maternity band, the sun's rays, the moon on which the woman stands, the 'angel' at the bottom of the image and her whole attitude symbolize the traditions of the Indians. The story also epitomizes the history of the indigenization of the Christian faith as well as the European–American cultural synthesis.

The archbishop is Mexican by origin and American by birth. He does not have to be convinced about the necessity of reconciliation among peoples. Will he, will the church be listened to by the powerful forces that are around, when he gives a preferential — 'though not exclusive' — attention to the poor and the powerless? Will signs of reconciliation spring up in 'Mexamerica' like the Guadalupe roses in bloom?

Take up your harp
That same year, on another tour, I needed silence. I walked into a small retreat centre in Berkeley. Especially in university cities there must be a need for places of silence, not only for the silence which is absence of discussion but that inner attentiveness which is praise, listening to a holy whisper, inner integration in a Heart in which we can centre down.

Trinity Methodist church created — besides the Bare Stage theatre, a Hand and Mouth Poetry group and a Spiritual Direction school — this desert three blocks from downtown Berkeley and three blocks from the University of California. A simple, empty house with six rooms and a chapel. I disturbed one person on retreat by visiting the upper room. I thought of Kierkegaard's warning: 'If I were a doctor and were asked for my advice, I should reply: create silence! Bring people to silence, the word of God cannot be heard in the noisy world of today. And even if it were blazoned forth with all the panoply of noises so that it could be heard in the midst of all the other noise, then it would no longer be the word of God. Therefore create silence.' But personally, I would dream of a simpler place without couches and soft rugs, something more dramatic, echoing the struggle against my discordancies, a place of wrestling, with prayer mats on the roof and my face in the dust. But even this little desert reveals to me that we all need to take time in order to create in ourselves wider spaces of welcome, to put spokes to the madly rolling wheels of our activities, imagination, statements, policies and to wheel around, to reconcile in oneself polarizing tensions in the Church, between the moral majority and the peace demonstrators, between the explorers of heaven-led lives and the down-to-earth fund-raisers, between the settled churchgoers and the wandering wounded, the suffering of the world and the satisfied First World. Silence is a combat for reconciliation. Only by reconciling in ourselves the purest intentions of all the groups, parties, classes, generations, sexes, populations, peoples and continents does Church emerge.

Think during your silence of the questions asked by the young people in the Greyhound bus: 'To what matters might you attend so that Christ would shine within you and through you?' There they are: Become a person newly born who trusts in God's love, who finds in him all the love you need. Leave detours. Be a source, a festival for people. You have friends, you have met witnesses. They stand on the horizon. Mist hangs in the air. Morning comes. Take up your harp and gold bowls filled with incense. Your rider is called 'Faithful and True'.

3

Building up
Community

A key word one hears today is 'connectedness'. People feel 'disconnected' from one another and from the world because of the impact of modern technology, inner alienation and individualism. A Presbyterian minister admitted: 'We've got all those activities, but who needs them?' When I asked him how we as church could be a place where we breathe God's presence, he explained that he integrates activities as a way of reaching people, as a way of building community. The old church died, he said, because they did not have that sense of belonging to the community, nor did they create it around them; 'They were not connective.' 'And it keeps being confirmed in my mind that that's what all these folks are looking for.' Why? Because so many feel fragmented and alienated. 'They probably don't put the term "God" on that. God is not controversial. God is just beside the point, but I'm talking about the hunger that I think is there.' Community organizers say that Jesus healed people, enabling them once again to enter into relationships with others. They believe that the parish has tremendous potential as a place of communion, a community of communities, where a forceful solidarity with the problems of the neighbourhood can originate. It is the brokenness of the poor that motivates the effort to link up parish and neighbourhood. Here is the way the Archbishop of San Antonio describes America's eighties: 'I have seen the empty gaze of families who don't have enough to eat or enough to live on. I have seen the bitterness of fathers who work and work and work and still cannot provide the necessities of life. I have felt the futility of children who go to school but learn so little. I have seen the anger of people who feel as if life and opportunity have passed them by. I have seen the sad and hurt looks of children from broken homes, the epidemic of crime and violence, the tragic results of addiction to drugs and alcohol.' And therefore he calls for 'a new Pentecost', for a new community of disciples in which the barriers of separation are broken, in which unity and diversity are both essential and in which the poor discover dignity and hope.

The new neighbours
In 1977 three brothers of Taizé, including myself, had been asked to explore the possibility of starting a small American community either in San Antonio, Texas, or in New York. The idea was not so much to start a new branch or a foundation of Taizé but rather simply to be present among the poor, to be a sign of joy and friendship, to listen to what people are going through and to pray, without knowing beforehand where it would lead us. No organized institution, but a 'house of Nazareth' where the Risen One is present and where people can come to share and to pray.

What city can compete with New York? We ended up in New York. But we spent a good and intense time in San Antonio, living for a month in a poor neighbourhood on Travis Street, close to Buena Vista. When I drove through the neighbourhood the other day, I didn't know any longer exactly where the house stood. I found myself in the situation of someone who, in an old village, tries to find the home of his youth. Every house looks the same, and the inner compass trembles without pointing out any specific direction. But then it happens that something deep and hidden in yourself recognizes an atmosphere, a climate. That happened to me on Travis Street. I jumped out of the car to see Mr and Mrs Calderon who had been our neighbours. In 1977 it had taken some time for the three of us to be understood. Three men, coming into the neighbourhood, renting a house, praying three times a day with a lot of people who came to join them, not only from the neighbourhood but, in impressive cars, from the North Side as well as from out of town . . . We had converted the room at the entrance of the house into a chapel. There was a young woman from the neighbourhood with a crystalline voice who sang the Our Father. We did the readings in Spanish and English. On Sundays we went to Sacred Heart or, on the East Side, to a small black Baptist congregation with an old minister who asked us to sing between the offerings (there were many of them, I remember). Everybody in the assembly had some liturgical function and walked around at one or another moment of the celebration. We sang in Latin 'Benedictus qui venit' in three voices. At the end of one service, there was a loud and terrifying dispute among some women in the back of the church. But the minister, like many old black ministers, seemed on his Olympus from where he could oversee the gathered souls beyond the clouds. The joy of the Gospel had indeed accompanied him so much during his long lifetime in the midst of distress and oppression that it was sufficient to look at him for your own evangelization. What he said did not seem so original or logical (nor what an acolyte told us in the Bible study before the service, during which we — the only pupils — had to answer his questions). He didn't need words; somehow the very origins of the mystery of suffering and hope had become transparent in him. During the week we had numerous conversations all over town, with community organizers, the six-parish coalition, the Mexican American Cultural Institute, our friends at Madison Square Presbyterian Church, and the Divine Providence Sisters. We understood something about Mexican American roots: the roots of 'a long way to nowhere, unwillingly dragged by that monstrous, technical, industrial giant called Progress and Anglo success', in the words of the poet 'Corky' Gonzalez. The roots of Aztec civilization, of Cuauhtemoc and Netzahualcoyotl, the roots of 'my Indian sweat and blood' given for Spanish masters, the roots of that 'lasting truth that Spaniard, Indian and Mestizo were all God's children'. The roots of Mexican history, from the freedom from Spanish rule to the parasites who remained to Don Benito Juarez, guardian of the Constitution, the roots of the bloody revolution. During its peak the Chicano movement in the United States led Mexican Americans to recognize much of what they are. And first the name itself. They named themselves Chicanos; nobody else gave this name to them. Today those between twenty-five and forty, in so far as they have not yielded to the lure of complete Americanization, like the term Chicanos. A new image other than that of self-pity has helped to sustain their identity as Mexican Americans. Like all the movements of the sixties, this one, too, is no longer as visible or impassioned as it was, but it has uncovered roots. 'We start to move, La Raza! Mejicano! Español! Latino! Hispano! Chicano! or whatever I call myself, I look the same, I feel the same, I cry and sing the same. I am the masses of my people and I refuse to be absorbed. The odds are great but my spirit is strong. My faith is unbreakable, my blood is pure. I am Aztec Prince and Christian Christ. Yo perduraré! Yo perduraré!'

But we also simply lived in the neighbourhood, trying to be part of it together with our neighbours. Mrs Calderon had finally warmed to us and brought us tacos or complete dinners. We felt like Buddhist monks who collect their food in the streets. But, finally, we had to leave San Antonio.

We quickly became New Yorkers. Rootless, New York catapults itself into extremes. The future sweeps the place like the ocean winds rushing through Manhattan avenues. In the Southwest old Spanish Missions witness to antiquity, although they have degenerated to outlying remnants without actual relationship with the city that has gone astray. Dallas shows rebuilt ruins of a bucolic farm from a hundred years ago, standing out in solitude, last symbolic centre kept up by the city fathers, in spite of the inner city highways and high-rise colossuses. For a New Orleanian — even if he

leaves it entirely to the four or five million tourists a year —
the only imaginable centre, the mythological cradle of civili-
zation, is the French designed *ensemble* of symmetrical
streets between Esplanade Avenue, Rampart Street, Canal
Street and the river, with its Jackson Square and the St
Louis Cathedral facing the Mississippi. Even for
'Americans' living in Fat City in Jefferson Parish and the
suburbanites in Metairie and in New Orleans East, the
Vieux Carré is a mythical Ispahan, although nowadays
their pride builds like everybody else from Houston to
Edmonton Superdomes and One Shell Squares. But New
York is a twenty-four hour Babylon where skyscrapers disappear overnight and drills sculpt out of rocky materials the
semblance of a crystal city. New York is constantly re-
fashioning itself according to the pattern of the winners, like
a chameleon changing its colours or a serpent-goddess with
a thousand skins in her parlour. New York needs well-
springs. Doves more than serpents. Places of quiet, faces of
charity, lives of tenderheartedness. We found a niche on
48th Street around the corner from 9th Avenue in quint-
essential New York according to Steinberg's poster. And we
asked ourselves: how can we be a neighbour in New York?
How can we as a small community, how can the Church in
general, be rooted in the reality of its neighbourhood,
vitalized by the neighbourhood organizations, yet remaining what a small community, like the Church, is called to
be, heaven on earth?

We wanted to navigate between Scylla and Charybdis.
Scylla: Somebody high up a ladder was talking to me while
at the same time an 'artist/activist' was explaining why fifty
colourful banners five foot nine inches long and two foot six
inches wide were hanging down from the ceiling. A Presbyterian church? I could have sworn I had walked into a
community centre. Were there not some remains of wooden
pews up front? I felt sad. Is it necessary to immerse a church
so completely in neighbourhood activities in order to attract
people? Is there no longer today a hidden longing for God, a

desire to be rooted in God even if people are not presently capable of discerning it clearly? Should the Church not rather be remodelled — perhaps just as thoroughly as a church emptied out because of a banners exhibition — that God can be met? One small room is kept free as a quiet space, and even that room is used for many other things. Nobody comes in to use it as a meditation room, though they have a sign on it that says: 'Meditation'.

Charybdis: On the moving scene of the city, with its clashes and struggles, a monastery stands immobile on an avenue. At the entrance I hear a voice coming out of the dumbwaiter asking me who I am. The voice gives me directions through the corridors to a parlour where I wait as if facing iron bars in prison. The open spaces between the bars in the rather dark room are so small that I can only get a glimpse of the persons I'm speaking to by curving my neck, yet each time I do this, it seems to me as if the Sisters look around the other side of the same bar — and we miss one another. The Sisters complain about the materialistic culture that prevents young people from living a life of sacrifice. I say, on the other hand, that although many young people are indeed preoccupied with self-gratification, self-preservation, self-interests, I have met a lot who among the ruins of the eroding post-industrial society are still able to be concerned about people outside of their own immediate circle. As a matter of fact, in spite of TV, affluence, the loss of the sense of duty, patriotic identity, fading work ethos, historical ignorance, apathy, I'm amazed about the emergence of people and communities living out a real solidarity with the victims of our age, in Central America or in prisons or in the face of nuclear threat. I tell them about the hundreds of young adults taking part in the weekends of our pilgrimage of peace and reconciliation, almost all involved in a search for their vocation or ministry in communion with the Church.

Two extremes of Christian presence . . . We have been inspired by a new ecclesial current that does not turn the

Church either inside out or outside in. This new style emphasizes, rather, the mutual link between parish development and community involvement, one sustaining the other. Certainly, we need both of the extremes sometimes; the parish, however, somehow has to balance different ecclesiological elements in order to be a sign of the Church for people who, in most cases, will not encounter any other sign than their own local congregation. It seems to me that this osmosis between parish and neighbourhood can be seen in many places, in different stages, without, however, representing a co-ordinated movement. In Chicago I recently discovered some interesting examples of this dynamic relationship between parishes and their neighbourhood that today can be found in many denominations all over the United States.

A Catholic example of the neighbourhood focus is Holy Family, next to the University of Illinois complex. The parish is run by Jesuits. Started in 1857, the parish has seen many waves of immigrants. Mother Cabrini, when she founded hospitals in Chicago, worshipped at Holy Family. There is a statue of her in the church. Each ethnic group has left its mark on the church. St Patrick stands on the front main pillar parallel to St Ignatius. Several statues of St Joseph, the patron saint of Italians, are around. One of the side altars is dedicated to Our Lady of Guadalupe; the other one has a black Christ in resurrection. Today, through shared events and through a shared parish council, the Jesuits try especially to create a sense of friendship along racial lines between blacks and Hispanics. Each year the feast of Our Lady of Guadalupe on 12 December is prepared in common by the Hispanics and the blacks — the music, the readings and the food. It has become a festival to celebrate their unity, and it is called the 'unity Mass'. The local community organization under the auspices of Holy Family has been revived since the parish picked up this independent organization, which was in decline. West Side Catholic churches have always supported local organizing efforts, in the tradition of the Archdiocese and its office of Urban Affairs. Today, a parish like St Pius in Pilsen, the former Czech and new Mexican neighbourhood, is even directing a community organizing effort through the churches. At Holy Family one is very attentive to the necessity not only to fight the city in crisis situations (housing, crime, and street problems . . .) but also to sustain the struggle indefinitely and to become a sign of an alternative system of values. Already the leaders of the local community organization were gravitating spontaneously towards the parish, out of a need to ground themselves in the reality of sharing among families and in a theology of suffering. Those people who are ready to fight look to the Church as a place where a new image of a reconciled society can be lived out in advance, through lives of friendship, mutual support, attentiveness to senior citizens and to school children. As one of the Jesuits says: 'If Holy Family were not here, many would either move away, seeking the good life, fleeing to the suburbs if they could make it, or they would give up. This church makes a difference to this neighbourhood.'

Among the Lutherans lots of things are going on, not only on the level of some congregations, but in the very reformulation of their concept of the local church. An opportunity for a new vision is given by the fact that three Lutheran churches (the Lutheran Church of America, the American Lutheran Church and the Association of Evangelical Lutheran Churches) are in the process of merging. Only the Lutheran Church of the Missouri Synod has backed out. What will be the result of the unity between the Lutheran churches for their pastoral ministry? In some places, for instance in Philadelphia, it will not make too much difference, since there is only one ALC church in the city. All the others are LCA. In Chicago, there are sixty LCA congregations, twenty-two ALC and nine AELC congregations. Altogether the new church will include—just in the city—about a hundred congregations. They are located in all parts, North, Northwest and South. Some of these churches are on the same blocks.

Historically, Norwegians, Swedes and Germans had to have their separate churches, not unlike the national parishes of the Catholic Church. The traditional way of doing ministry has been to have one pastor for each parish, unless a church was very big and had more than one pastor on its staff. The new orientation is now to see how to yoke congregations and to put together ministry teams that include the staff of different congregations. Lay people can join them, part-time or full-time. The Lutherans see this, not as a way of diminishing ministry in one particular congregation, but on the contrary as a way of strengthening ministry. If one pastor serving two congregations has a lay professional who focuses on a particular area, time is then freed for the pastor to do some more concentrated work in other areas. On the Northwest Side, for instance, there are two congregations that remain separate in their identity but have a joint staff which includes one pastor, one intern, and two part-time lay people. One does Christian education while the other is involved in community organization. The parishioners thought, at first, that their pastor would become part-time because he was going to work in two congregations. But they see the pastor more now than they ever did before. He is finally able to centre himself on certain areas. When the Lutherans come together, they will be able to make this a general principle, particularly in areas where the congregations from the former churches are in very close proximity. Why are these structural realignments important? Because the Lutherans want to use this opportunity to focus their pastoral care on the neighbourhoods in which their churches are located.

Normally, in Protestantism, people swarm from wherever they live, even if it is fifteen miles away, to 'their' church on Sunday morning and sometimes during the week. The congregation as such is not involved in the neighbourhood, because only a very few people live there. This is especially true for inner-city congregations consisting of rich people whose church is located in a neighbourhood that is becoming poorer and poorer (the Catholic approach is much more geographic; each Catholic parish is present in the neighbourhood). The Lutherans in Chicago are now trying to educate and to train their pastors and lay people to see the parish in geographic terms. Everyone within that particular geographic area, within that particular parish, is the responsibility of that pastor and that congregation, whether they belong to the congregation or not. That is not to say that they intend to steal people away from the nearby churches. In my opinion, however, this concept needs to be explained clearly to other denominations in the same area so as to avoid fears and competition and to move together with the other Churches toward a real ecumenical approach in their evangelization efforts. In this concept the parish has a responsibility for the people who reside there, not only for their spiritual well-being, but also for their social, economic and financial well-being. The parish needs to know the people, their hurts, their concerns, and their needs.

During a certain period, coinciding with the exodus to the suburbs, a number of denominations decided, or were forced, to close down their inner-city churches. The property sometimes was sold to a bank or a hotel, and new churches were built in the suburbs. I remember having seen the shameful carcass of an Episcopal church on Philadelphia's West Side. It was filled with leaves fallen from nearby trees, covering the pews waiting for the breath of the Spirit. The Lutheran churches in Philadelphia committed themselves to the inner city, in spite of the people who had left. The twenty parishes that are part of the 'centre-city parish' have very small congregations, but they have the strength of a community church, standing there with open doors. The pastors, quite naturally, had to lose the management style others are used to in busy, ultra-active congregations and to deal with the question of the lack of 'efficiency' of the church. What do you do when there is no success any more — work frantically or retire? In Philadelphia I found a style of presence — a prayerful presence — lived out among the people in the neighbourhood. The pastors walk around in the streets; they know the people. The only thing that shocked me was the fact that they resembled Catholic priests (Lutheran pastors wear a Roman collar); I wonder if this does not confuse the people. Unconsciously, there may be an attitude of *'cuius religio, illius religio'* ('we are the priest in this section, they are in the next one'), while an ecumenically shared ministry, especially in the poor inner-city neighbourhoods, seems to be so evidently necessary. Chicago is very different from Philadelphia. The Lutheran Church in Philadelphia has a predominantly black constituency, the Lutheran Church in Chicago a predominantly white one. By 1985 they hoped to reach 17 per cent black, 3 per cent Hispanic and 0.5 per cent Oriental. In Chicago, the Church is not flying high in terms of congregational membership or economic growth, but it has, on the whole, not suffered the decreases like the Lutheran Church has in other major metropolitan areas. The LCA in Chicago is probably the strongest. In Philadelphia there was no choice other than to tell the people that a change had to be made. In Chicago, the Lutherans do not have their back against the wall yet, which means that parishioners can still remain reluctant to change their understanding of what it means to minister and to go into the community and be a part of it.

The choice, however, for neighbourhood ministry has been made. The Lutherans have congregations in all kinds of communities that are ethnically and racially different. If the congregations reach out and are faithful in sharing the Gospel with the people in their communities, the Lutheran Church throughout the city of Chicago will be a very inclusive Church. That is not to say that there will not be some entirely black or entirely white congregations, since in reflecting the neighbourhood, they will reflect Chicago's divisions. When the Lutheran Church in Chicago as a whole comes together, it will represent the variety of Chicago's population because the congregations are located in those different communities. They don't look systematically for integration everywhere, but for a ministry to all the people within the shadows of their steeples. As a result, the Church will reflect what is there. When they see an area that in its cultural and racial characteristics is not represented within their church, they start a new congregation, e.g., a Chinese congregation on the North Side or a Hispanic one in the South Lawndale area.

It is essential to make collegiality in neighbourhood ministry possible among the pastors. The pastors have to be accountable to one another and for one another. That means spiritual togetherness, coming together to study the Scriptures and common reflection about joint programming. Out of these intertwined options, many other avenues of involvement will open themselves, particularly those supporting the role of the Church as a witness in the public sector. In so far as ministry is seen as an involvement with people on all levels, one cannot help but make statements to the city government about whatever needs have to be advocated. The Lutheran Church is going to work together with community organizations. But grants are not enough; there has to be local involvement as well. There is no network of community organizations in Chicago that could speak out, as such, to the City Council, as is the case of the coalition of neighbourhood organizations in Philadelphia or of the UNO in Hispanic East Los Angeles. Until recently, it was a Jesuit who headed the umbrella organization in Philadelphia. Why couldn't some well-organized Chicago Lutherans start a similar coalition in their city?

Much of the history of Chicago has been the struggle of groups for a just place within society. Each immigrant group — in order to make it on their own — settled in a neighbourhood; they tended to regard the others with a very low level of trust, simply because at first they had been refused. As long as they remained second-class citizens or servants, society still accepted them. But on an equal basis? There have always been clashes between the different ethnic groups. For the blacks — who were immigrants in their own country, forming almost 12 per cent of the total American population — the struggle for justice to overcome discrimination and apartheid between neighbourhoods has been dramatic. Chicago is a city of strong conflicts. Parties, groups, neighbourhoods don't work in coalition. 'A city that works', setting people against people, victims against victims? Or a city that works for justice and righteousness for all the people involved in it, working in coalition with other groups? The influence of the Churches on the life of the city is still very important. Could that influence be used to promote coalitions, righteousness, justice? Over the past twelve years an organization like the Campaign for Human Development has supported many peacemaking groups, community organizations, low income housing initiatives and reinvestment programmes throughout the Chicago area. If all the churches together would see this as a priority in the second part of the eighties, would their influence in that case not flow from the roots of their own life?

Another important aspect concerning the link between local churches and neighbourhood involvement is the significance of liturgical life in a parish that involves itself in the neighbourhood.

The liturgy discloses that other world which we can't obtain by our own efforts, however generous they may be. It is, therefore, not surprising that the neighbourhood involvement by American churches takes place in those denominations where one can find a contemplative and liturgical life. Especially in America's inner cities, blacks, Hispanics and many other poor feel at home in churches that are bathed in twilight, where candles illuminate the sanctuary, processions cross the aisles of the nave, and choirs fill the air with music; where the sign of the cross, genuflection and the red lamp are allowed to sustain personal prayer; where chapels with statues attract visitors; and where the atmosphere fosters a subtle interior but very real emotionalism in the liturgy. The osmosis between parish development and neighbourhood involvement, sustained by an intense liturgical life, leads not only the parish into the neighbourhood but also allows the neighbourhood to recognize the uniqueness of their church.

Most of all, however, we have been inspired and confirmed by a paralysed woman on our own block in New York. Rushing through the city, flying from one city to another, coming back to the city and leaving again the next day, we thought often of her as our reference, as an icon of truly Christian life in the hurly burly of New York. Twenty years at her window on 48th Street had made Frances Carpenter a landmark in the neighbourhood. She had not led an ordinary life. As a young girl she was struck by paralysis. The disease had never been diagnosed. In the fifty years which passed since the morning that she couldn't get out of her bed, she raised an orphaned nephew and nursed her parents at the end of their lives. Until 1975 she was able to get around in a wheelchair, but from then on she was mostly confined to bed. Young and old, her neighbours paused on their way to and from homes, jobs, outings, to say a few words to Frances. Her life was not lived in isolation. She could not walk away. For several years an elderly Italian lady, the immigrant mother of Frances' landlord, used to come and sit by her bed for a few hours every morning. The old woman would talk non-stop, recounting the dramas which had filled her life, crying, laughing, sighing, but all in Italian because she didn't speak a word of English. Frances laughed and cried along with her for years, even though she didn't understand a word. She was full of nostalgia for the past and love of the present. 'You'd be surprised how nice the people are in this vicinity.' Her family was of great support to her, especially her niece Betty and her cousin Elizabeth. In addition, she received daily housekeeping help from a young woman who was paid by the city. Her front room, which overlooked the 48th Street Block Association Garden, was the meeting place for her tenants' association. 'I wouldn't live in any other place if you gave me a million dollars.'

'I've known thousands of people. I always try to treat them nice.' Her simple, gentle way brought out the kindness and gentleness of those who came into contact with her though she was robbed three times and once hurt. Hers was a life of welcoming, so much so that to Frances no one seemed a stranger. During the long years of vigil at her ground-floor window, she listened to the secrets of many souls. Her main concern for those who came to her with their problems and complaints was to find a way to encourage them. She loved children and was often asked to baby-sit. Frances had no thought out principles to expound. When asked for advice, she responded spontaneously, without method. What she said came from her heart.

From the familiar way that Frances talked about Hell's Kitchen, it sounded like a small country town. For many people her presence on the block made walking on 48th Street a homely, neighbourly event. Often a priest from Sacred Heart came to celebrate Mass in the apartment of this unique woman. On one wall there was a reproduction of a stained-glass window depicting Saint Francis of Assisi at home in the forest. Upon seeing this picture, one of her neighbours remarked, 'We have our own Saint Frances'. It is sad that she passed away after a lifetime of smiles. We still walk by and we convince ourselves that Frances' transfigured face is indeed not with us any more. It is now up to us to light a paschal candle in the neighbourhood.

On 48th Street we meet together, preferably on a Friday evening, for a prayer around the cross. In the room which serves as our chapel, we place on the floor an icon of the cross, surrounded by candles. We sing a song like 'Stay with us, O Lord Jesus Christ, night will soon fall; you stay with us, O Lord Jesus Christ, light in our darkness', infinitely repeated, sometimes louder, sometimes more softly, according to our inspiration and the strength of our breath. It is a form of prayer which has come to us from Eastern Europe, where young people began to pray in this way at a time of persecution, in communion with their friends in prison. It is a liturgical prayer which is centred on the Passion of Christ, a Good Friday prayer. At the end of this prayer each person goes up to the cross, and rests his or her forehead on the wood of the cross to entrust to Christ the burdens of all those whom he or she knows, and all that personally weighs them down. Each person comes forward in this way, silently, while the others sing.

I imagine that each person experiences this prayer differently, and each time in a different way. But living where we do, one cannot help calling to mind the face of those youths on the corner of the street who sell drugs to the people of New Jersey in their beautiful cars; the faces of the girls of our neighbourhood, sometimes bright, at other times hard and wounded; the face of Frances, beside her window and then the faces of those men and women whom we haven't known how to honour, whom we have wounded or ignored, attacked, or avoided. We see again these faces which live in us, and then we go to the Risen One who, in his Passion, enlightens and heals, brings calm and new life to the features of our own faces. I believe that in this way, in the midst of the faceless city, clusters of light are passed from one to another because of the communion of Christ. And, inevitably, actions spring forth from this, according to our capacities and abilities. We ourselves have been led to set up a tenants' association, to enter into negotiations with the city in order to legalize our situation as squatters, to throw ourselves into the housing problems of our neighbourhood, to work with the elderly, with young prostitutes in the area, with seamen from the third world, and to welcome all kinds of people into our home.

One can easily feel guilty in regard to the city. The city has become a jungle; happily, some things still work, whether because of habit, laws, self-interest or all the investment we have put into it. But that is all. Pope John Paul said in New York: 'The city is in need of a soul.' Let us become a reconciled community, in order to awaken, in the hearts of all those around us, a vision of a city of compassion.

97

Catalysts for justice

What is the rationale or ideology behind the imbrication of parish development and solidarity with the neighbourhood, an imbrication whose elements seem to overlap one another like roof-tiles in so many places in America, in Chicago but also in East Los Angeles, San Francisco, Brooklyn's East New York, Baltimore, Houston, El Paso and most particularly in San Antonio? How do the consultants and community organizers, hired by the churches, express their concern and purpose?

Parishes, wherever they exist, the organizers argue, are usually small islands in the neighbourhood where people meet, only on Sunday, for an hour, with other people whom they don't really know. The parishioners don't feel any particular responsibility for the neighbourhood in general; specialized organizations that have nothing to do with the church take care of its problems. Congregations and families, however, suffer in their life as Christians. They suffer in the education they want to give to their children; they suffer from all kinds of aggressions around them that undermine the foundations to which these congregations and families would like to witness. These often quite subtle forms of aggression oblige them to ground their existence on secular and materialistic values. They come from a world determined by the developers, the insurance companies, the banks, the blind face of urban bureaucracy, in short by a subtly, perfectly organized power that has profit as its ultimate aim. Would it be possible, building upon the traditions of the neighbourhood, to balance the power of the institutions and the power of wealth that reign in the neighbourhood with the power of the people, the families, the parishes? Would it be possible, for instance, to convince a television station to make a film about the drug dealers on the street corner next to the high school as a way of pressuring the police to do something?

If a parish organizes itself so as to become a place of peace and justice in the neighbourhood, if, with the help of ecumenical contacts, actions are undertaken together with other parishes and congregations from the same neighbourhood, then there will also be hope — the organizers say — for an intensification of the life of the parish and the groups and the movements that are part of it, hope for a new perception of the parish as a 'body', as a place of sharing, hope for a renewal in the spirit of the beatitudes. (In the training sessions led by the Industrial Areas Foundation — the consultant agency for this kind of community organizing in cooperation with the churches — frequent references are made to the beatitude of the meek. Meekness is interpreted as . . . anger, in terms of strength, on the basis of an exegesis which reformulates the beatitude as: 'O the bliss of the man who is always angry at the right time and never angry at the wrong time'!)

Bringing people together in a neighbourhood is an effort that takes much time and that demands from those who initiate it a lot of patience, listening, the capacity to entrust responsibilities to others and a rootedness in the spirit of the Gospel. But how practically to bring together a neighbourhood? First, one should contact the local priests and ministers. What are their opinions about the problems their families and congregations encounter? Who could be the laypeople in the parishes one could meet in order to reflect with them upon this same question? What are the pressures put by the institutions and other powers on the life of the people, especially of the poor? What are the priorities of this group of clergy and laypeople? Together with them a group of eight to twelve people could be built up, to ask the same questions of others and thus to enlarge the group of interested people. After some time, the most interested people could meet and choose one topic, one problem that is not too vast or too intertwined with other problems, and then they could involve everybody, encouraging them to read, to do interviews and so forth. A knowledge of the facts and of the existing documents is most important. Some could ask the city for the official models that are used to redesign the

99

neighbourhood; others could find out about the hidden command structures and learn more about the decision-making process. At the same time, the house meetings would continue. Later, it will be possible to set up larger meetings and to choose a group of people to co-ordinate the whole search-process and action. Soon, the co-operative effort in the parish and between the parishes, the effort to integrate all the generations, will be intensified. One day it will be possible to have a group of fifty to two hundred people who will really represent other people, groups, organizations, and movements. Then people can come together, as soon as an opportunity arises, for a large meeting or convention and speak out about a specific issue concerning the neighbourhood.

The organizers are very much aware of the fact that those who would commit themselves to such an effort will be confronted with a lot of difficulties: Will the priests and ministers consider it really their business? How can one find laypeople able to take on responsibilities? Will this educational experience for adults be really attentive to the poor and the elderly? Will they remain attentive to the limitations of this new structure and keep the spirit of the Gospel alive? Will the participation really activate the people? Will there be a vision in order to keep the groups going?

This whole community organization process has been most successful in the city of San Antonio, Texas, where COPS (Community Organized for Public Services) has intertwined itself with the Catholic, Mexican American parishes on the West Side. Its methods have become part of the parishes' revitalization program in the archdiocese. During the last few years the movement has branched out into the North Side. Compared with the West Side, the North Side is a totally different territory. You move from a slum to utopia. The green hills of the far North Side, the wooded environment, the omnipresent shopping malls, the conformity in classism and racism, the homebuilding boom, the economic exodus of the city's business activity out of downtown to Loop 410, the closeness of the airport — all this has led to an important growth pattern that has conquered almost all the land available beyond Loop 410 out to Loop 1604, in the direction of the Hill Country. Job locations as well as commercial and residential development have centred almost exclusively on the North Side which is evidently detrimental to the East Side, and indeed to the West Side, where 34.8 per cent of the population is below the poverty level and the unemployment rate is above 30 per cent. It was in the middle of 1980 that the organizers were able to unite a certain number of churches on the North Side in the Metropolitan Congregational Alliance (MCA), distinct from COPS out of respect for the differences of interest between the people on the North Side compared with the other parts of town.

There is, of course, clearly in everybody's mind the perspective that in the future the leaders from different parts of the city might work together in order to see if a common strategy could be worked out. The integration of strategies is a long-term goal. To put it more bluntly, pedagogically the North Side has to go through a process of awareness, starting with a reflection in the congregations and parishes about the role of the Churches in society and verifying the results of these reflections in small actions. Then it will be possible to build up a federation and to confront certain issues together across the whole town. The basic purpose of the MCA is precisely to call the Churches to leave their ivory towers and their concern only for their own constituency and institution. The MCA calls the parishes to discover the Church, broad and universal. In the MCA there is implicitly this dynamic for linking the North Side churches with other neighbourhoods in the city and for building up a network of people, power, money and leadership that would facilitate concrete solidarity beyond the North. This direction has not yet been officially formulated, but it is implicit in the inclusion in the same organization of member churches from other parts of the city, especially from the South Side. In many cases the MCA will not even address issues of self-interest for the North, preferring to give information to help people decide questions concerning the West and the South Side. Already now, the North Side members are becoming conscious of and working with the South Side and, through COPS, with the West Side. The vision behind the creation of the MCA is the city as a whole, so that issues and concerns bring all San Antonio together instead of having people always divided.

In general, community organizations, like all movements, don't last much longer than five years, unless they accept to institutionalize themselves. COPS made it and got beyond the fatal deadline. But they are working with the poor who feel the need to get organized and to receive help. On the North Side the organization has not yet taken off. A lot more work has to be done within the congregations. The MCA also needs a broader base than the fifteen individual churches which comprise it (Lutheran, Presbyterian, Methodist, Disciples of Christ and Catholic; the Southern Baptists keep to themselves). Up to now the alliance has remained predominantly Protestant and has been less successful with the Catholic parishes on the North Side. The organizers estimate that it will take three more years to get seriously organized and to move into important issues on its own.

In fact, critics on the North Side address themselves primarily to the tactics, the aggressive, confrontational style, rather than the issues. Certain issues have been the same on the North and the West Side: the water issue, the discussion about San Antonio's growth pattern, the city's public services, the rights and costs of utilities. More recently, they have addressed together the problem of a nuclear powerplant that should be on line in 1989 in Bay City, near Houston.

According to the methods used in parish development, in which three or four geographically proximate parishes take part, the very first session in the meetings with the parishioners confronts the question: what is the meaning of the Church? Reference is made to St Paul in the First Letter to the Corinthians, St Paul who protests the misuse of the celebration of the Eucharist in Corinth because it leads to separation, because the rich get drunk and nothing is left for the working-class poor to eat, because the local Corinthian culture is brought into the celebration, and so forth. What are you doing with the body of Jesus? St Paul is asking. The same question now resounds in San Antonio. One of the reflection processes is to have people pretend to be St Paul, writing to the Body of Christ in San Antonio. People who up till then were unconcerned or resigned come up with fundamental questions: Why are you separated from each other? Who don't you become one? Where is the new creation you are supposed to be? The Christians in San Antonio have taken on the culture of America, have not critiqued society; they have acted in a secular way, along the lines of the white middle-class mentality, isolating themselves, taking on the values of consumerism and materialism. The Mexican Americans as well have isolated themselves and have let fear dominate their lives. In that situation the basic Gospel message is the call to break down barriers, to cross over the lines of division. An organizer told me the example of a bond election that took place some years ago. The hundred-million-dollar bond was badly needed for a drainage project on the West Side. The discussion became so political that the bond was defeated, not because it was not a good one, but because racism became the paramount issue. The question became: who is going to have the power in San Antonio: the white Anglos or the Mexican Americans? 'The crime of that election was that the local parishes and congregations on the North Side did not speak out and never helped the people to interpret what was happening.'

The archdiocesan parish development approach and the COPS/MCA methodology are intertwined by the very fact that the same people head both avenues of leadership.

There are, however, tensions. First of all, not all the priests are in favour of it. COPS/MCA, on the other hand, officially invested with this responsibility, insists that parishes remain active and follow through, calling on priests and asking them to preach and to explain the parish development goals: to visit homes, to find leaders, to find needs, and then to train leaders, and to plan response. COPS, in spite of the emphasis on using democratic, people-oriented methods, employs, for efficiency's sake, a hierarchical stick. They want to use whatever authority is at hand to reach their goals. The Archbishop will speak out on city issues — not frequently enough for COPS — but he does it in his own way, without having consulted with the COPS leadership. It is over the different views of power that tensions come to light. The whole purpose of COPS is to call forth that power which is within people to bring about justice, but in the Church today, at least in San Antonio, there is a hesitancy to build its ministry on the use of power. Because of the very clear vision in the COPS movement concerning the implications of Christian faith — some call it 'political moralism' or 'sectarian attitude' — there could one day be a conflict between the COPS ideology and the priests, if they ever decided to choose another pastoral direction. Here and there people say that one day the organizers will recommend dropping the clergy. But the pastor at Christ the King on the West Side is very positive: 'COPS has functioned as a catalyst to get people out of a simply vegetating attitude. People have found confidence in the Church because of COPS; the Church can now begin to mean something to them.'

COPS thinks that change comes about on the basis of mutual self-interest, power and the result of pressure and threats. COPS brings into the Church political methods that run the risk of 'instrumentalizing' the Gospel, as the Italians would say, of making it a tool for their own purposes. This does not mean, of course, that there should be no space in the churches for the community organizing concerns. It means that the community organizing approach should be balanced by another movement, a movement of reconciliation. As much as there has to be defence of the poor, there should also be struggle for reconciliation. The word is absent at the present time in their terminology, which is made up of concepts like anger, power, organizing, success, threat, strategy, and tactics. Could there not be a similar movement, just as penetrating, dynamic and liberating, towards reconciliation? What is the 'new Pentecost' (title of the Archbishop's pastoral letter) that could be blown into the life of the whole Church in San Antonio that would integrate the liberation of the poor into a global vision of reconciliation?

It is only around the peace issue in the context of the national debate that Church leaders in San Antonio — Anglo, Mexican, Black, Baptist, Methodist, Presbyterian, Episcopal and Catholic — have been able to write a common letter. Why would it not be possible for the leaders to sit down together regularly, keeping in mind that as one Body of Christ with a common responsibility, no decisions should be made without the others? The hesitancy to consider other baptized persons as full-fledged Christians who belong as well to the Body of Christ prevents us from making the decision to share everything together, joys and struggles as well as the common task of evangelizing and renewing the face of the city. San Antonio is dramatically impoverished because of this continuing division.

I drive to the 'San Antonio Light', a newspaper building, where I want to find in the archives an editorial which I vaguely remember that was published some years ago. I run from one floor to another until I find the archivist in a little room without windows. He keeps news stories and editorials that were published in *The Light* in little yellow envelopes, stuck together in an apparent order in old-fashioned files. After a while it seems to become a hopeless investigation, until someone remembers that the article I'm looking for was published in a special promotion issue. That

105

means I have to go to another floor. Several people are now on their knees looking through old baskets. 'Never mind,' I say, because it's awkward to see people work for you, and I make my way to the elevator. But then somebody shouts 'Eureka' from inside a closet full of clothes hangers and coffee spoons. The title of the editorial is: 'Many faces of San Antonio prove we *should* be one face' and I find in it exactly the message I would like to apply to Christians who are called more than anyone to live out parables of communion. 'The challenge is that, in our diversity as a people, we can find the strength which leads to unity . . . Can our four cities be one? . . . This city finds strength in diversity of cultures and ethnic pride. We believe not one of these cultures or one of these ethnic backgrounds should be dominant over another . . . Abraham Lincoln warned us against divided houses. As divided nations cannot stand, neither can divided cities.'

Would that language be unimportant for people involved in community organization efforts who want to rewrite the letters of Saint Paul to the people of our time?

Unity in a nutshell
In the United States, the ministries taken on by parishes and congregations reflect, in most cases, the insights of the individual pastor or staff, insights nurtured from an attentiveness to the concerns of the congregation. Among parishes and congregations there is no uniformity in the pastoral approach, not even within one denomination. This does not mean that parishes oppose one another, although in many cases there may be some competition. There is often no co-ordination. In Paris the pluralism of ministries in the Catholic inner-city churches was officially decided some years ago, along the lines of what individual churches already had been emphasizing: ministry among students, a church for liturgical renewal, a more contemplative church, and a church to minister to intellectuals or Latin–American political refugees. In the old Anglican churches in the City of

106

London around St Paul's Cathedral, a similar distribution and specialization has taken place, inspired by the necessity of palliating the shrinking interest of Londoners in those Anglican churches, churches admired more for their architectural value than for their ministry. Is there a danger that by assigning specific roles to local parishes, ministries may simply be juxtaposed, needed cross-fertilization may be lost, and the universal aspect of each local church may be diminished? In Paris and London at least complementary ministries were implicitly recognized. Nowhere have I seen a completely ecumenical approach, an attempt to put all the pieces of the Church's jigsaw puzzle together. Yet only together can the ministry of the Church be made authentically present.

Arriving in Sweden recently in the Scandinavian winter, one of our first impressions was seeing candleholders in all the windows, crowned with flickering lights. They are put there for Advent, following an ancient custom. One morning at Harnösand, in the north of Sweden, we left the house very early to go to the cathedral to pray. The car was sliding on the snow. Coming down the hill we could see the whole valley lit up by these candles. So many little lights in the darkness of winter! One little light: a shared parish council composed of Lutherans and Syrian Orthodox Christians in Vallby, a satellite city on the outskirts of Västeras. Around many Swedish cities, satellite towns have sprung up in recent years. These satellite towns, planned on a uniform model, offer all that is necessary but people do not like living there. Many apartments are left unrented. A significant proportion of the residents are immigrants, living there because they have no other choice. In Vallby the immigrants are Finns and Turks. Among the Turks a certain number belong to the Syrian Orthodox Church. They have been persecuted by the Kurds, another minority in Turkey. In the sanctuary of this new Lutheran church, located in a former furniture factory, one finds an iconostasis rebuilt by the Lutherans who travelled to South East Turkey in order to be able to make a copy of the original one. They showed us their sacred books, written in Aramaic, the language of Jesus. We went to pray with them in front of the iconostasis. The liturgy is celebrated in the morning and in the evening; in between, Turkish men sit down in the Lutheran 'open house' and help to welcome alcoholics. Decisions concerning the life of the parish are made by the Swedes and the Turks together.

In America I saw beginnings here and there. Unfortunately, co-operation or unity are often only the result of some organizational simplification, founded on the latest management techniques rather than on the desire for visible unity. Sometimes churches in the city are looking for ways to meet a problem that every downtown church in any large city encounters: the problems of transients, emergency needs of people coming and knocking on the door of the church and needing help. Shared ministries are envisaged, using a common building, employing a supervisor and involving volunteers from the congregations. But the congregations involved continue to coexist. On the other hand, although the ecumenical reality in neighbourhoods is still in its early stages, it could be deepened quickly. When openness to one another grows and there is a willingness to become a catalyst for the neighbourhood, then such an ecumenical presence will flourish. Three examples may indicate a way of pursuing the search for visible unity on the level of the neighbourhood. To me the churches on the Northwest Side of Chicago seemed perfectly complementary in their ministries; why don't they share everything together? At Christ the King in San Antonio the need for evangelization becomes the incentive for openness to others. As soon as there is this consciousness of being vulnerable and fragile, the Church is seen again in her deep vocation as a place of communion for all. The Sather Gate churches in Berkeley found each other through a common involvement in the sanctuary movement.

Although Logan Square on the Northwest Side of Chicago is not a microcosm of the whole city, it is certainly a diverse area. There are no very rich or very poor people. The upper-middle-class executives are still young and only climbing the economic ladder. Most are lower middle-class people who put everything they have either into the house they own or into their savings account. Their savings are not in stocks and bonds; they may have a five figure balance in a passbook account. Black people live in Logan Square, so it is an integrated neighbourhood, but the poor are white Appalachians. There are many ethnic groups but the Hispanics are now the majority (53%); together with the young executives and the German and Scandinavian old people — the Lutheran remnant — they form the main categories within its population. There are very unusual churches in the area. I saw a Polish Baptist church. Pentecostal churches are surfacing. Not far from the Episcopal church of the Advent is the First Liberal Psychic church. The Christian Science church has gone out of business. A new Mormon Temple, a multi-million dollar operation, was built in the area. One evening, I meet with a group in order to reflect upon ways to increase and broaden co-operative efforts between the churches. All the people gathered see the churches' role in the neighbourhood as a catalyst in the community, bringing a sense of community between the executives, the elderly, and the Hispanics, especially for re-building the neighbourhood organization. We meet in the Lutheran parish, St Luke's. The church's main ministry is to the senior citizens, and their future is not clear because they have not developed a Hispanic ministry as the Church of the Advent has done. In the meantime, many things are going on in and around the church. A major option is to open the doors and to be very much a community-oriented church in which people gather. Thirty organizations use their facilities, from alcoholics to a dog obedience school. Young people, mainly from poor white families who don't want to be part of the youth gangs that gather around Humboldt Park have started to come to St Luke's. Their programme is called GRIPS (Growing Responsibly Into

Persons). Ministry to them is done together with the senior citizens. This intergenerational work normally starts with entertaining each other and grows to sharing with each other. Sometimes there is a crisis, especially when there is a peak of vandalism in the area. But communion between the young and the old seems to be growing. Together they started an intergenerational kitchen band; sometimes they take the band out on the road, visiting other churches.

The Episcopalians and Lutherans in this area are working closely together. They both emphasize very different and complementary facets of ministry. They don't duplicate each other's efforts. They didn't sit down and plan this; it just happened that way. The Church of the Advent, for instance, besides the Hispanic ministry, has a pre-school day care centre which is badly needed in the community. It also sponsors General Education Development classes, classes in English as a second language, a narcotics anonymous group — all ministries the Lutherans can benefit from. But the other churches could also be included. Fourth Congregational Church is into clothing. St Lucia's has a food distribution centre. At St Luke's they also have a food pantry of canned goods for hungry street people. The Advent takes a collection every Sunday for this ministry at St Luke's. St Luke's and the Advent block the street off between their two churches on Palm Sunday, and they do the liturgy of the palms in the middle of the street. At least a certain number of the ministers from the area come together for prayer. But they have not been able to bring in the Pentecostals, and the Catholics are less involved. However, St Nicholas, a United Church of Christ involved in the nuclear disarmament issue, the Fourth Congregational Church, the Polish Baptist Church, and a Spanish Congregational Church are all part of the prayer meetings. What a witness would it be when each church brought its gifts to the others.

Christ the King, on Perez on San Antonio's West Side, is 99 per cent Mexican American. The parish does not belong to the six-parish coalition west of Chambers, but COPS is definitely present in the *barrio de Cristo Rey*. For the people here, the main issue is evangelization. The story goes that some time ago the Archbishop went to the Convention Centre Arena for a meeting and found the parking lot packed. What's going on here? Why are there so many people coming? he must have asked himself. He walked to the part of the Center where his meeting was to be held and saw people passing by who either didn't recognize him or, more likely, didn't want to say hello. Finally, he spoke with a couple. They told him that they had been Catholics but were now Jehovah's Witnesses. Since then a renewed effort for evangelization has started in the archdiocese. In the neighbourhood around Christ the King, the Jehovah's Witnesses are not present; on the contrary, the many non-Catholic churches represent the Church of the Nazarene type of church. The pastor at Christ the King recognizes perfectly the difference between Jehovah's Witnesses and the Protestant denominations; he knows people who, having converted to Protestantism, have enriched their prayer life, increased their knowledge of the Bible and really become Christians. Although, as in all Protestant churches, many who attend on Sunday come into the neighbourhood from very far away — because of the minister or because they have grown up in the neighbourhood — many others come from the neighbourhood itself. It is not true any more to say that the West Side or that the Mexican Americans are Catholic. Many of them have grown up without having been baptized. It is not possible any more to say that they are even nominally Catholic. The West Side is not Catholic. There are lots of unchurched people. According to the pastor, the credentials of the Church are still accepted. The church is not yet lost in the *barrio*. 'But we have to reach into the real *barrio* soon' and to affect their community life.

In a closely knit neighbourhood like the West Side all kinds of neighbourhood communities exist, some somewhat Christian, others not at all, where people express their need for and their joy in communion. There are little icehouses,

111

for instance, where every Friday afternoon men and women gather. Maybe seventy-five per cent of the same people come back every Friday afternoon for fellowship and sharing: 'One round for you, one round for me'. They exchange jokes, and they talk about the events that have occurred in the past week. 'There is more communion in that ice-house than it is possible to find in the church. The only communion we make available is the Eucharist. In many ways, we are selling Jesus down the drain and expect him to be what we are not doing.' Then there are all the coffee groups and the across-the-fence groups of women. 'We are not providing a sign of unity on the church level.' 'We are not connecting them. We are not helping with that connectedness which we need in society.' At the same time the people not only find communion in the ice-houses and the coffee groups, but they spend what they can't afford on that communion, while at home the kids are the ones who suffer.

COPS connects people, opens the horizon, awakens the people but has not yet reached the really poor. Not only the organizers, but also the volunteers and the members, are middle-class. It is, therefore, a challenge for the parish to build on whatever the community organization has accomplished. The people believe in what the community organization leaders have done, but what is the next step? How can they become part of the community of believers in Christ? The same enthusiasm, the same awakening has to happen on another level, another rung. The neighbourhood has found confidence in the church because of COPS; the church can now begin to mean something to them. COPS is connecting this neighbourhood to others through a quid pro quo system: this year we are doing this street, next year yours; you push for us, we push for you. But if all they do is to make better streets available, people will simply travel faster through the *barrio*. That does not change the in-depth quality of life. An alternative is given through the community organization, but now they need to go further and, having taken care of their environment, take time to reflect upon their relationship to God. It is time to intensify what COPS is trying to accomplish and to build up a community of believers, not only of activists.

One sector of the parish does not relate at all to parish life. Some people have started to meet in that area, on a weekly basis, to read the Scripture of the following Sunday. The purpose is to make it possible for more people to have a sense of belonging to the church, not necessarily connected with the parish as such, until the day they themselves choose to join. The aim is not to shore up the parish structures but to make an intense church life possible, a community of believers in Christ with an ecclesial dimension but without an immediate connection with the parish. Fifteen *communidades de base* exist in the parish. They all study the Bible and base this study on the reality in which they live. They ask themselves questions like: What can we do as twenty families together? What is our responsibility as believers? To what other community of believers do we reach out? How can we set up a system of visits by going to one another's homes and becoming apostles to one another? Some of these questions can easily be linked up with the community organization issues and could deepen them. Group members design liturgical celebrations and pray the funeral rosaries. Other ministries could emerge, freeing the priest and enabling him to become the link between manifold initiatives. While the *comunidade de base* is a family of families, the parish could then become a wider community for celebrations that could help to transcend all the problems inherent in small communities. The common worship could be stronger because people would have learned to celebrate in small groups.

The Church has always involved itself in a prophetic service by assuming responsibility for health care, education, and youth organizations. Although the new communities still have no visibility at Christ the King, the seed is planted on the parish council level. They think it is time for new communities in the church today. 'If only the *comunidades de*

113

base could offer communion to the people. Communion is the bottom line of humankind. In our life in this neighbourhood, communion is what we are all about.'

Berkeley, California, is ecumenically a very rich community because theological seminaries here are joined in the Graduate Theological Union and because the so-called Sather Gate churches (the name of the south gate of the university) are working closely together. Representing all denominations, they are located within a three-block area. The clergy of five of the eight parishes meet together every Tuesday morning for Bible study. Frequently, the same sermon title turns up in all the parishes. This trust between the pastors, built up over the past years, is certainly one of the key reasons why they have been doing so many things together including initiatives concerning Central America, an emergency food project and the University Religious Council (a common organization for campus ministry). Back in the fall of 1981, one of the items that was in the news very frequently was the sending back of Salvadoran refugees living in the Berkeley area to El Salvador. The churches came together to see what they could do to stop the deportations. People were raising money to hire attorneys. They were talking to the airlines to agree not to fly the deportees. A few churches in the area offered 'sanctuary', an ancient concept that is adapted today in several places in the US (Tucson, Chicago, Milwaukee, Portland, Oregon). In those churches people put themselves between the refugees and their deportation. Some of these churches had done the same thing for people who were refusing to go to Vietnam — helping to hire attorneys, building up communities of support, and taking people into the church buildings. In 1982 the Berkeley churches signed a 'Covenant of Sanctuary', interpreting sanctuary as 'support, protection and advocacy' and offering to surround the refugees with concern and care, even if it would be required that they move into the church buildings. They recognized that legal consequences could result from their action.

114

Because helping them as undocumented refugees — they were not recognized as political refugees — could conceivably be considered a felony, the churches were involving themselves implicitly in civil disobedience. The churches were Presbyterian, Catholic, Lutheran, Methodist, and Episcopalian. Later on, another Roman Catholic church and a Quaker meeting joined. They say it was a tremendous educational experience for the parishes. At the same time they decided to ensure a continuing presence of international visitors in the refugee camps in Honduras, sending a delegation every two weeks. Every other Sunday night, at least two people go to live for a couple of weeks in the refugee camps in dangerous territory. When they come back, these people are, of course, the core of committed workers who are able to handle calls for individual assistance to refugees. As soon as there is a common ecumenical involvement in what is happening in the world, it is not surprising that a link is made with what is happening in the immediate community. An example is the Berkeley Emergency Food Project which feeds a hundred and twenty people a day. Mostly younger people come, many of them have psychological problems or are unable to find work.

For us in New York, it is very important to be linked with parishes. I know just how boring a parish can be, mundane, desert-like, rigid, out-of-date and discouraging. And yet it seems to us that in New York a parish is the one and only place where men and women of all ages, of all ethnic groups and all races, and of diverse opinions meet together, or should I say, could meet together, for other than commercial reasons, because of a common search along the line of the Gospel. Here and there little communities are springing up. They have a time of enthusiasm and are immensely appealing, although they often have found no way to go beyond the circle of friends all of whom have roughly the same ideas and have no real contact with the poor. In our neighbourhood lots of groups and root-communities do exist; how can we begin together to perceive the parish as a community of communities?

A little dream: in our neighbourhood in New York there is a tiny Presbyterian community, another of Episcopalians, another of the United Church of Christ, one charismatic community, and another of Indian Christians, all of them minuscule. Many of their members have a Catholic background. There is also a large Catholic parish, with Anglo Americans and Hispanics. Might it be possible that one day each one, understanding the other as a different spiritual family, and without denying the richness of our diversity and of our identities, could link itself to the Catholic parish, which would become, so to speak, the 'cathedral' of the neighbourhood? Who more than Christians are called to establish in a neighbourhood a network, a framework, a chain of relations, links of love which are capable of supporting so many other people?

I find an unexpected ally in Herman Melville's *Moby Dick* (Chapter 18): 'What church dost thee mean? Answer me.' Finding myself thus hard pushed, I replied, 'I mean, sir, the same ancient Catholic Church to which you and I, and Captain Peleg there, and Queequeg here, and all of us, and every mother's son and soul of us belong; the great and everlasting First Congregation of this whole worshipping world; we all belong to that . . .'

4

Belonging Together

Christ's robe was made of one piece of woven cloth without any seams in it. The churches, however, give an incredible *dementi* to the prayer for unity on the eve of his death. Although the dazzling diversity of Christian institutional manifestations is also a sign of effervescent fervour and untiringly renascent creativity, where's the simplicity of the Gospel? What has happened, in the cacophony of ever multiplying church structures, to the archetype of the community in Jerusalem, meeting in the Temple, selling their property and possessions, distributing their money among all, eating with glad and humble hearts, and learning from the apostles?

Christians belong together. Although our common belonging produces a vertigo, although there is no end to it, Christ's prayer calls us to conversion, to the reality and visibility of an authentic communion. Why repeat the separations of the past? It is time for a revival of reconciliation. 'If you are about to offer your gift to God at the altar and there you remember that your brother has something against you, leave your gift there in front of the altar, go at once and make peace with your brother, and then come back and offer your gift to God.' Everybody in his or her ministry can find ways to unity. Everybody can be a hidden reconciler. Reconciliation is not very far away. People work at it, more than one would believe. Who will measure their efficiency? In the hidden history of the Church, people unravel entanglements, lift up heavy-loaded burdens, knock down unruly resistances by longing for Christ's fulness in his Body. '. . . so that you will know how very great is his power

117

at work in us who believe. This power working in us is the same as the mighty strength which he used when he raised Christ from death and seated him at his right side in the heavenly world. . . . God gave him to the church as supreme Lord over all things. The church is Christ's body, the completion of him who himself completes all things everywhere' (Eph.1.18–23).

Let us commit ourselves as people of God, as local churches to the search for reconciliation, in communion with the woman in prayer painted on the fresco in the catacombs, with Jehoshaphat and Uzziah, Ahaz and Amminadab, Azor and Zadok, the astrologers and the shepherds, with Mary Magdalene weeping beside the tomb, and all the other women who have seen and heard, with the monks sitting on pillars in Egypt or eating grasshoppers in the Sahara, with St Francis dreaming of the reconstruction of the Church, with Hopeful and Christian looking for the way to the Celestial Gate, with artists and dancers and acrobats with all the millions of poor people who have suffered and who in the midst of their confusion have rested upon the faith of the Church.

Let revival and reconciliation go arm-in-arm

Does the word reconciliation belong to the vocabulary of the religion booming in America today? Revival, renewal, return to religion, rebirth, yes; reconciliation, I don't believe so. Sociologically speaking, it is an established fact that any church, whenever it is in a minority situation, lacks breadth and has a tendency to show a certain narrow-mindedness. Far out of the mainstream one fears that the larger bodies will eat up the small remnant that keeps the whole truth in a nutshell. Way out in the desert one feels like the last Indians who have to defend even the last square feet of land they had been allowed to live on. In their meetings adherents are challenged to find their strength in isolation. As soon as a denomination is in a majority position or is comprised of equal numbers, however, openness grows, generosity comes up more easily and naturally. This is like a rich man, sure of his ease, who can give liberally of his wealth to those poor fellows who somehow should have at least a minimal living. Numbers, assets and prestige seem to reduce the alluvia of antagonisms that had almost eroded the common ground shared with the others. But does that generosity lead to reconciliation? Does the search for reconciliation not imply recognition of the others in their uniqueness, a sense of common belonging, willingness to witness together?

In Texas, the Southern Baptists have five million members. The congregation I visited is a booming church. On the first evening, invitations to come back on Sunday or to speak with the ministers were issued generously with each handshake; but it seemed to be improper to try to pin down right away one specific appointment for the coming week. Maybe one is first expected to confirm the seriousness of one's interest by showing up another time at one of the gatherings, before the well-meant welcome can be translated into that kind of incarnation which is the negotiation, agenda in hand, of a convenient time and place. Beforehand, while asking for a tape, I had noticed this formality. I was told that I had to be introduced first at one of the gatherings. Unfortunately, this very week there would not be a regular prayer meeting. This formal attitude seemed in contrast with the extremely relaxed way in which I was sent from one pair of hands to another towards the table where I was finally allowed to sit down. I must say that the person who introduced me, and who was at the time only a recent member of the 'fellowship', did not know much more about me than that I was the friend of a friend. The unmistakable difference of being inclassifiable and my inability to explain in a few words my whole story and the reasons for my presence at the gathering must have produced an inner conflict between the evangelical thrust of Christian hospitality and the human restrictions of prudence and unawareness. I am not sure that I did not in some way oblige the friendly minister to whom I had been delegated to see me; in any case, he did not seem to remember the exact time of our meeting when I stood in his ante-room the next day trying to convince his secretary, who was at the same time trying to calm down a busily gesticulating lady with an urgent prayer concern. We succeeded finally in working out a schedule, after I explained that I would not take much time because my driver was waiting in the car outside. When I finally sat down on the couch, I tried to remember what I had come for.

There are obstacles when a person searching for ways of reconciliation sits down together with a minister involved in a fast-growing congregation, not yet (or no longer) permeable enough to receive the necessary input from Christians who are different. I was puzzled to find myself pushed into the role of an interviewer. There you are, sitting in a room, ready to welcome the other, whom you hope would have liked to welcome you with all you represent and to share together. Already the time-limit weighs upon your openness like a sword of Damocles; at any time a reason can emerge justifying the interruption or the end of the conversation. But then, the very silence of the other person forces you to explain why you are both there, looking at one another. The silence has to be filled with worthwhile questioning that optimally would help you both to forget about the time and arouse in the other at least a question or a sign of recognition or interest, so that you both will leave the room at a silently negotiated moment, with some gratification and happiness about the fact that you were able to overcome the barriers between you. To answer the silence by silence would have led to an awkward confrontation. Questions had to be spread out on the table, but by accepting to do so, the risk is that the answers will be self-defensive autojustifications, thought out in an in-group from which you are excluded and spoken out of an ivory tower of power. At the opposite pole there would be a sharing attitude in which one's vulnerability, struggles, failures and hopes would become transparent, out of the insight that we are involved in a common search.

Baptists are widely respected in this town, I say, but they seem to give the impression of wanting to be insular in the ecumenical movement. Well, says the minister, last Monday evening the pastor was master of ceremonies for a gathering at the university, in which, for a cross-section of the community, there were denominations of all faiths: Roman Catholics, Lutherans, Presbyterians, and Methodists. It was the presenting of a man with the name of Colson who at one time was in the Federal government, was convicted of having had a part in the cover-up that dealt with the administration, found the Lord when he was in prison, and now has dedicated his life to a movement helping those who are incarcerated. This movement addresses itself to everybody, and the Baptists are very much a part of it. They do not join, however, in common worship with the other Christians because there are some points which the Baptists do not believe are at the heart of what the New Testament teaches about the Gospel of Christ. How could two walk together if they do not agree? How can you walk together if one depends on something with which Baptists cannot agree? It seems to me, I say, that in many places potential relationships between Christians never materialize because of the impossibility of accepting the others in their differences. Only sameness, only uniformity in doctrine as well as in congregational lifestyle would make co-operation possible. In society in general, in organizing efforts for example, an emphasis on intuitive values is opposed, or at least seen as a complement, to the oppositional, polarizing style. More and more voices say: try to look for support from others rather than trying to control them; humanize society; bridge gaps among people; try to stand with the oppressed; find solutions to community problems which allow all parties to win; focus on positive signs and on the strength in people and institutions rather than emphasizing negative elements. At a workshop at Mundelein College in Chicago, people talked about the historic moment in that city for moving toward values like compassion, softening, rounding the hard edges as opposed to the masculine imagery that would have reached its maximum and that naturally would have to move in the other direction now. These new values could lead, they said, to a fuller understanding of life and relations. They thought that the election of a Black mayor had been a significant step in this regard. How much more Christians are called to new relationships of communion and to a ministry of reconciliation in the midst of all the harsh divisions that surround us!

Well, says the minister, through the Baptist Association Baptists attempt to reach out to all the sections of the city, through mission activities and various types of programmes. Furthermore, people are sometimes like water and oil; no matter what you may try to do on a social basis or on an ecumenical basis, they are not going to be in the truest sense joined together. Others just won't care anything about being with other people. They are more comfortable with folks that they know, folks that either have the same ethical, ethnic or social background, or the same something else. You do not build great works in trying, in a determined effort, to mix them. People are like water; they need to be allowed to seek their own level, and some of them can be much happier in one setting than they can in another setting. That doesn't mean that any of them ought to be deprived. In this congregation everything is done to reach out to them, to minister to them, to share with them, to teach and to train. If they would like to, they may even become part of the fellowship. But that is not a condition. Some will join, others will remain where they are, and yet be helped for whatever they need.

Proselytism is certainly, I say, completely contradictory to the insight that the others are part of the same Body of Christ which does not belong to us but in which we, too, have been incorporated. Proselytism destroys trust, inspires fear, creates fights over people's souls and, above all, breaks to pieces our common witness. On the other hand, every church wants a full house and some money in order to survive. Catholics do fear evangelization among their own co-religionists in Texas. In order to prevent mistrust and misunderstandings and on the contrary to march towards more visible unity, should there not be initiatives on the Catholic side or the Baptist side so that at least small groups of people would meet and reflect together, making manifest the unity of Christ in the midst of those fears? Well, says the minister, there's no particular effort being made. There are so many people out there who do not know Christ. Instead of our finding so much time to break down each other's walls, the main thing is for all of us, in every way we can, as harmoniously as we possibly can, in the spirit of Christ, to continue to reach out to those who do not know him. And with regard to what manner we do it, just be sure that we're representing the Gospel of Christ, and not some order, or some church, or sect; just be sure that what we're reaching them with is the Gospel of Christ as we see it in the New Testament. That's what we're concerned about, and we're a whole lot less concerned about trying to knock down somebody else's doors, and we don't want to bar our doors to them.

The whole ecumenical thrust, I say, is based on Christ's prayer for unity among his disciples so that the world may believe and recognize God. To avoid the question of reconciliation between divided churches means to avoid becoming that reconciled community which through its very existence would speak of God's love, Christ's presence and the communion of the Holy Spirit. And doesn't St Paul call us to become ambassadors of reconciliation? Well, says the minister, a lot depends on what is meant by that. If it's reconciliation to Christ, it's one thing. If it's reconciliation as an ecumenical group, to an order or to a set of dogmas, it's something else. Baptists join with others in trying to bring about a reconciliation to Christ, a reconciliation through Christ to God. That's where their big interest lies. Everything else is subordinate to that. But St Paul, I say, speaks about unity between Jew and Greek, and about one baptism. Well, says the minister, Baptists just believe that. There are many co-operative efforts, and Baptists do not turn their back on any co-operative effort that has in it that vestige of representing Jesus Christ, and just because it may involve folks of other denominations, that doesn't bother them at all. But the one thing they want to be sure of is that the reconciliation effort is unto God through Jesus Christ, and that they're not just finding themselves out there, trying to prove their own way over his way. The main thing that's before them is the propagation of the Gospel. They don't think their churches have any justification for existence outside of that. And regardless of what form it takes, regardless of how it is done, if its primary and basic reason is not the propagation of the Gospel, then something would be wrong.

Walking back to the car I'm saying to myself that if such an admirable missionary dash were built on a solid ecclesiology, then revival and reconciliation would go arm-in-arm. Mainline churches seem to have lost the élan to announce the Gospel. How is one to be a missionary? Those reared in evangelical circles are convinced of the necessity to reach by all available means every single person, not only with a paper or the Bible or a flyer or a TV show but through a probing personal conversation, hopefully leading to conversion, to a choice. As a matter of fact, they would like to do that in the whole world and send missionaries abroad unto the ends of the earth. At the other extreme one finds people, as Christian as the others, who are searching for a new missiology not only theologically but with their very own existence. They favour an 'in-depth' approach, which means a witness to the Gospel given personally and in community, a witness rooted in prayer and intercession; they would leave it to the Holy Spirit to use this and through them to attract other people who ask themselves why these people are living in a different way.

There is much confusion among people between these two extreme positions. Some think that the witness model is too easy an escape from the commitment a Christian takes on himself or herself to announce the Gospel. One sometimes feels a certain suspicion that those who engage in silent witness are not sure enough of their faith. The witness people accuse, silently, the others of making out of the Gospel a publicity product that has to be sold at the highest price, with the greatest benefit. A third group sees mission much more as the vital concern for people in the city taken in the totality of their life. We shouldn't, they say, extract from them a 'yes' they may not have really meant, conditioned by solitude or distress, but become a lasting presence to them by involving ourselves in the struggle for better life conditions in the city, clean air, repair of potholes, clean-up of the subway system, and open-air concerts and by fighting against crime. In this context, they say, we can freely admit the motivations which lead us to do all this. For them, the Kingdom should not be synonymous with spiritual welfare, as if the Church would have hand-outs ready for whoever is in need of a meaning for life; it should lead to a continuous search for and a total rebuilding of a society along the lines of the beatitudes. I know people living in high rises searching right there for new ways of witnessing. The first thing they did in one of those towers was to find space for a chapel. Furthermore, by starting tower-associations as a defence against the landlord and by meeting with the neighbours in the elevators, by visiting with some families (those at least who don't close the door out of fear), they tried to build up some rudiments of a village life. And once a year a fair was held on one of the main avenues. People came out of their homes to look at old books, junk goods, thrift-store leftovers, foreign-food stands and electronic gags. That day all the Christians were on the street trying to make connections and also simply enjoying this festival. They put up a lot of stands and had people available who were able to listen to the life stories of their neighbours, to talk about the Gospel, the Church and neighbourhood concerns. But I believe unity of the Church is a precondition for evangelism, and evangelistic efforts lead to awareness of the scandal of divisions among Christians. Competition among Christians, getting a full house while hurting other churches, polite coexistence while keeping a measured distance are not works of the Spirit. Unity, reconciliation are. How could one imagine the Holy Spirit, the Spirit of communion, inspiring a time of evangelization and conversion in competition with other Christians and without the calling to become ourselves a visible sign of love, joy, peace, patience, kindness, goodness, faithfulness, humility, and self-control?

Revival is no longer credible when the search for reconciliation becomes secondary. It is the drama of Christian history that revivals led people to walk away from other Christians. Revivals led to new divisions. During the First Great Awakening in the eighteenth century, only Zinzendorf issued a call to unity during his stay in Philadelphia. Between January and June 1742, presiding over six out of seven Pennsylvanian religious gatherings, he dreamt of an association including Christians of all denominations — Schwenkfelders, Quakers, Sabbatarianists, Mennonites, Lutherans and Reformed Christians. But he failed. Even Wesley, who had the same passion for the conversion of the Indians as Zinzendorf and in spite of the fact that the revelation of his mission took place in the small Moravian community on Fetter Lane in London where he came to pray, separated himself from Zinzendorf. George Whitefield, the revival preacher who wherever he went between Boston and Savannah gathered thousands of people, attacked Zinzendorf, although the Moravians had helped him in his ministry with the orphans in Georgia. Zinzendorf had tried in Philadelphia to express the fundamentals of Christian faith, more important than the divergent opinions of schools and sects. In a sermon on Galatians 1:9, he said: 'There is only one foundation which is the

126

merit of Jesus. There is only one way that leads to life; that road is the knowledge of God made manifest in the flesh. This God should be preached, this God crucified, because crucified he has expiated and redeemed our sins. This doctrine contains all wisdom, all justification, all sanctification and all salvation. He who believes this is elevated above every other science; he who takes this with him into the other world is fit for eternal life. It is difficult to believe in it but not impossible, because the Lord, by his blood, has obtained for us all the capacity to believe.'

Do we live a time of revival today? On a rainy Sunday afternoon in Chicago I decided to go downtown to make a pilgrimage from church to church. At Fourth Presbyterian church on North Michigan Avenue the doors were wide open. The church was silent and I stayed a moment. The space reminded me of the original Cistercian churches, completely bare, where nothing is explicitly religious but where the space itself in its warmth, enclosing and uplifting, forms a kind of solid foundation on which all that comes on top of it can rest. In the history of the church a baroque or extravagant architectural style has inevitably been followed by a reaction of minimalism. Calvinist churches, that now appear to us as boring classrooms, had originally that same character of simplification, of poverty to which architects and theologians wanted to return. But at Fourth Presbyterian I wonder if it is enough to show stones, as if they communicate God, rather than the presence of people who by their very welcoming presence would shine some light in the dark atmosphere of their church. Would it be too much for a church in an area where people like to walk to organize some welcome, to hand out hot soup or cold tea according to the seasons, to have some families around who could welcome and lead into prayer the lonely pilgrim or the curious visitor? I walk a few blocks over to the Episcopal Cathedral, but it is hermetically sealed. Churches are locked more and more often because of vandalism, lack of people who watch what is happening and the custodian's schedule. At the heart of London, at St Martin in the Fields, street people sitting or sleeping in the side pews watch with their otherworldly smiles over the elegant, often scandalized tourists who visit the nave. My next station, at Holy Name Cathedral, is different. Such life! The office for marriage and family life has sponsored a golden wedding anniversary Mass. The church is packed. I am just in time for the recessional hymn, 'Now thank we all our God'. The old couples have just renewed their wedding vows. Fifty years ago they stood in front of another altar and promised that they would commit themselves to each other, in joy, in pain, in sorrow, in success, for the rest of their lives. That road must not have been easy for all these people. And here they are back. The archbishop speaks of the sign of their commitment: 'God has been there in the darkest hours, in the deepest joys.' Renewing their promises the couples, first the husbands, then the wives, have just said in front of everybody: 'We have been growing old together, we have together seen good times and bad, sickness and health, we have watched our children grow, we have seen our love deepen. I will stand by you now, and I will love you all the days of my life.'

I decide not to stay for vespers, to continue my little ecumenical pilgrimage and to head for the 'undenominational' Moody Bible Institute on North LaSalle. Their buildings look like a bastion. A pamphlet at the entrance says: 'MBI's distinctive stance is rooted in its history and a unique foundation in Bible fundamentals and financial support'! MBI has six hundred employees and fifteen hundred students on campus in order to prepare young men and women for communicating the Gospel. But it is not at all limited to the ages between eighteen and twenty-five. From kindergarten through to older adults, more than 105,000 students are in training each year. There are day and summer collegiate programmes in Chicago, evening school on the college level in eight cities across four states, a correspondence school, and a kindergarten in Florida. And besides education there is publishing (Moody Press, Moody Literature ministries, *Moody Monthly* and one book called *Successful Soul Winning*), broadcasting (owning and operating eleven commercial-free radio stations and producing programmes aired on more than four hundred stations world wide), Bible conferences held in St Petersburg, Florida (with heated swimming pool, shuffleboard courts, a scale model of Herod's temple and lots of concert evangelists — among the announced speakers, all male, one is designated as a 'twice-born Jew'). MBI says that American Christian schools are dead: Harvard lost its original view of the knowledge of God and Jesus Christ as the principal end of life; Yale's once evangelical stand faded away; Princeton secularized; other schools drift. Moody Bible Institute stands where it has always stood, in the steps of the founders, Moody, Torrey, Gray, Houghton, Culbertson: 'Our message is the tried and proven Gospel of Jesus Christ. Our passion is to see lost people converted and added to the family of God. Our motive is the constraining love of Christ. Our attitude is that of faith in a living Saviour who delights to do abundantly above what we ask or think. Our method is serving people.' I was invited to come back on Monday morning for the opening prayer in the auditorium and for a lengthy talk by the president about different ways to check God's will. What impressed me were those fifteen hundred young adults, lined up for prayer, singing the roof off the building and walking away with their Bible as if it would be their best friend. Do they live a time of revival today?

There is certainly at least a snowballing of evangelical religion in its immense diversity, mostly much more to the right than my Baptist minister. I'm in Texas and Jesus is all over. I'm driving to a housing project linked with the movement 'Habitat for Humanity'. On the 'Sonlight' radio Jesus music is broadcasted, blaring entertainment music with a religious sauce. Singers scream nostalgically pious songs over the airwaves. 'Je-e-sus knows just how I feel', 'I am redeemed, I am justified', 'I want to go home to the Fa-a-ther,

I want to go home, be daddy's girl'. Life is all smile and
smoothness. Hereafter it is enough to swing to and fro. But
many kids listen to this radio programme. Another station:
'Nine o'clock. No rain in the forecast. Tomorrow just like
today, beautiful and sunny all day long. Welcome to
"Classes for truth". One of the greatest scientists of our time
has said: How could I work on evolution for twenty years
and learn nothing from it? Evolution is not only not knowledge, it is anti-knowledge.' There are better things, 'Sounds
of the times', for instance, a campus interview produced by
Radio Bible Class of Grand Rapids, Michigan. And there is
worse. It is introduced in this way: 'It is never a pleasant
picture, the picture of war. During the next half-hour, so
and so will give some "insights for living" (title of the show)
about the war for the believer in Jesus Christ. He points out
this important truth, a truth we need to remember (and
now comes the Marine Corps voice of the famous teacher,
screaming). Whoever fights and loves it, is sick. Fighting is
not the kind of thing that brings man a sense of completion
and delight, if he is a healthy person. However, it is necessary for survival.' Then starts the movie music. The com-
mentator again: 'The subject of war is ugly. We think of nations against nations, fighting on the front lines with
weapons designed to kill. The Book of Jude, a postcard
long, speaks about another battle, just as gruesome as military conflict. It is the fight against apostasy.' Logopediatric
specialists on the Bible schools must have taught to pro-
nounce each word and to stretch it out for a second as a way
of emphasizing. The words resound in the air: sick becomes
sickkkk, the 't' of right gets an aggressive sound, and 'sub' is
pronounced with a hellish intonation. A line like 'we live
under the gun of secular humanism' becomes a violent
apostrophe that makes you shudder in your car. The last
quote of my florilegium is an American history summary,
the last message for the people in my car on the parking lot
of 'Habitat': 'When faith was first introduced to our land,
people believed what the first line of the 23rd psalm says:

130

The Lord is my shepherd. As humanism began to roll over from the old country and took its root here, we began to say: I am my shepherd. Then we began to believe it so much that we turned to: The sheep are my shepherd. And then: everything is my shepherd. And finally the bottom line: nothing is my shepherd.' Do we live a time of revival?

Newspapers are full of stories about classroom prayer, evolution, gun control, 'Does God Hear the Prayer of a Jew?', sexual preference, and soon the year 2000 will give an opportunity to millenarianists to come forward. The number one non-fiction best seller in the 1970s, aside from the Bible, was Hal Lindsey's *The Late Great Planet Earth*, which has sold more than 15 million copies. That many readers wanted to know what could happen to them on doomsday. Millions of Christians believe that an apocalypse is at hand and that possibly God will use a nuclear holocaust in order to stop the world. And because doomsday is near, we now need Christian schools of which there are already now twenty thousand. In St Louis a reporter told me that in Missouri more than one hundred and forty independent Protestant schools operate. In addition, eight hundred to one thousand and five hundred evangelical Christian families in Missouri are keeping their children out of schools and teaching them at home. 'A return to religion', 'A Revival of God' were 1984 titles in *The New York Times*. Statistics confirm this upswing. Gallup's telephone interviews with 1,029 persons turned up clear evidence of a revival of interest in religious and spiritual matters, especially among Protestants (among those expressing a religious preference, about 60 per cent). At least 64.5 per cent of them are more interested in religion now than they were five years ago. About 43 million adult Americans are actively participating in Bible study groups. Over the past five years the proportion of college students interested in religion has grown from 39 to 50 per cent. Do we live a time of revival? The same polls say, however, that the churches suffer from it; membership in organized churches has dropped from 73 per cent of Americans in 1965 to 67 per cent in 1984. The Sunday before the poll only half of those who identify themselves as Catholics were at Mass. Only 43.6 per cent of the professed Protestants were at church.

In 1984 the Sojourners in Washington, DC, expressed the hope for revival. They see a stirring in the churches, especially in the joining between personal faith and the struggle for justice, which is also their own emphasis in their ministry. 'The old divisions within the churches are breaking down — evangelism and social justice, prayer and peacemaking, spirituality and politics, worship and action, pastoral and prophetic ministry.' The Sojourners are themselves among those who have shaped a new way of living out the Gospel, in Biblical obedience and in social justice. 'Today', they say, 'America is bound by sin. We no longer trust in God but in our wealth and military might, and the fruit of our idolatry is a nuclear arms race that threatens the world with extinction.' Their hope is for an outpouring of the Holy Spirit. Soon, they will be on the road from city to city to preach and to 'call people away from the ruling American myths, illusions and lifestyle; from the sins of the people and the sins of the nation; from injustice and war; and from individual selfishness.'

How will all this affect the Church? The Church lies in pieces. It is as if faith, mission, justice have undergone many changes and developed with extraordinary dynamism since the old days, but the perception of the Church as the body of Christ was somehow left behind. Like children who mature physically but not spiritually and grow indifferent to religion, Americans seem to have left behind in their children's shoes the lesson about the unity of the body of Christ in the catechism of all ages, a lesson too difficult to learn on the new continent. Could the separation between Christ and his Body, the Church, be healed? Are bridges possible between seventy times seven churches?

We pray for revival. Please pray for reconciliation and let them go arm-in-arm.

Save the Gospel!

At the end of 'The social sources of denominationalism', H. Richard Niebuhr writes (in 1929!): 'Christianity as represented by denominations, which in turn are representative of the divided culture and its divisive interests, is no more able to stem the tide of disintegration in the world than it is able to set bounds to the process of disintegration within itself.' There is a need for the churches to rediscover their uniqueness in the face of a divided culture, the uniqueness of the Gospel that contradicts separations between groups polarized between poor and rich, black and white, and other divisive interests. The uniqueness of the Gospel is lost when the Church is used to confirm ourselves in conformity to the surrounding world we have grown up with or which we have consciously chosen. The Church has all those treasures for which people in the midst of their separations yearn: forgiveness, reconciliation, 'the vow of love of enemy and neighbor' (Niebuhr), repentance, sound eyes, prayer behind closed doors, and a life without revenge. The Church is challenged to project the reconciliation which is at the heart of the Gospel to a civilization that worships competition and admires only the winners.

In Chicago, racial polarity is not only the stigma of the fights that have taken place around the election of a black mayor. It is institutionalized in the whole urban make-up. I remember a visit to Hyde Park, site of the University of Chicago. Being close to Midway Airport, I took a bus east along Garfield Boulevard. It went through miles and miles of black neighbourhoods, stopping on each street corner, loading and unloading crowds of black schoolchildren with their satchels. I was the only white person on that bus. The driver gave me a sign as we approached Woodlawn Avenue. Although the neighbourhood is a little more heterogeneous than I first thought, I had the feeling of entering a kind of enclave, a middle-class oasis, a bastion of academia, walled off from the rest of the city. I was going to attend a discussion at Rockefeller Chapel about a possible student pilgrimage with participants from all over the Mid-West. The students in the area, it seems, are for the most part uninterested in the presence of all those neo-Gothic structures that border the street corners. Vocational problems created by a growing unemployment rate, competition for financial aid, part-time jobs, the competitive attitude that is imposed on them by the race for success, lead to an intellectual capitalism that cannot but exclude the joy of a community of faith and the peace of a time of contemplation shared with others. The churches are there, huge buildings donated by generous alumni, but who comes? The campus ministers now want to bring in a lot of students from elsewhere and to show to the students on this campus that something is going on in the churches. Is it a good idea to create such an event? They want famous speakers and leaders. It seems the students are only interested in famous people because they cross paths with so many of them at the university. I come up with the idea of englobing a wider area than Hyde Park and including neighbourhoods like Kenwood to the North and Woodlawn to the South, both black and poor. This would give the students the opportunity to leave their libraries for a while and to discover their less fortunate neighbours. They could spend part of the weekend with them, talking, eating and praying. Could that be one of the aims of the pilgrimage, I say innocently, to create links between the university and the poor who live all around it? For some reason my idea doesn't come across.

As a matter of fact, Hyde Park has used university money to wall itself off from the surrounding area. In the Woodlawn area the university has bought up much of the property and has simply demolished the buildings. Today it looks like a bombed-out area. One can easily imagine that the longer this sort of enclave exists within the city, the greater the animosity toward the people within the enclosure will grow. The Woodlawn neighbourhood is the one where Saul Alinsky, the radical community organizer, worked. Once he took four hundred people from Woodlawn, all very poor, primarily black people, to the First National Bank. Every one of them had a dollar. They all opened savings accounts. They just flooded the bank with busloads of people. The bank employees asked: 'Where are they all coming from?' They were told they were from right here, from Woodlawn. At that time they had a dispute with Commonwealth Edison over some question of pollution control. The president of Commonwealth Edison, the enormous utility company, had his offices in the First National Bank. Alinsky asked if they could meet with the man. The answer was no. So Alinsky threatened to come back the next day, to close every one of their accounts and to come again the following day to open them again. Of course, he got to see the person he wanted to see. But he did not succeed in his confrontation with the university. The land was bought up, the houses were destroyed, and Alinsky died in the meantime. Nothing has really been rebuilt in that area other than what the university needed for itself. The aim had rather been to have a buffer zone between themselves and all the other people around.

How to bridge this disparity, visible from one block to another? How to heal Chicago's chasms? Some people say that a shift is now taking place, that Chicago is changing in that people don't remain in their neighbourhoods any more. But this changing is done on the basis of wealth. They are rich and can then afford to move to other areas, but they will protect the property to which they move by keeping others out.

Another example of an enclosed area is Park Ridge, a suburb west of Edison Park, a few blocks from the Chicago city limits. It is a very wealthy section. People in Park Ridge fear that one day the walls around them are going to fall down whether they like it or not and that people of different races and different economic groups will be moving up in their direction. I asked several people if there are any blacks at all in Park Ridge. Somebody remembered having seen a child of mixed racial background in the street once in a

135

while. Being the first black to move in is awfully difficult. There are other suburbs, comparable in wealth or even richer, that at least have a token black population and maybe blacks who earn the same amount of money as people in Park Ridge who first migrate in those directions rather than breaking fresh ground. Park Ridge, being an old suburb, has certainly a different mindset than the newer suburbs. The Northshore, often considered more liberal, has a number of blacks. Park Ridge is Republican and conservative. The median salary of the people is approximately forty thousand dollars a year. The country club has a six thousand dollar initiation fee and annual dues of three thousand dollars.

The racial polarity which coincides with the rift between poverty and wealth, the haves and the have-nots, certainly creates a great deal of suffering, anguish and sorrow in Chicago. Sometimes it manifests itself in anger, sometimes as despair or brokenness. In New Orleans I looked a long time at the train station, trying to imagine those trainloads of black people, enticed by advertisements in the 'Defender' offering jobs in Chicago, who left for the Midwest after the Second World War. The white community advertised in this black newspaper that was passed from hand to hand. The blacks went to Chicago thinking it was the promised land. But that hope was dashed; that dream was never fulfilled. The sorrow in the people stems from the lack of fulfilment. They thought they would find in the industrialized city of the North everything they could not find in the South. Their dreams not only concerned economics; they also believed in the possibility of escaping racism. But Martin Luther King called Chicago the most racist city he ever encountered. In the South, blacks knew in a certain way where they stood, but now they were not even sure any more if this or that white person they met was really honest or not. How could they belong to a culture and a society they were both part of and *not* part of? How can you find your place if you don't know what to expect and, therefore, end up expecting the worst? Today, because of the economic situation, the gap is getting wider and wider. Many blacks say that their situation now is worse than in the sixties. A greater and greater polarity is developing in the city.

In the face of the separation between all those diverse and often desperate groups, the Church's vocation is evidently to serve as a channel by which reconciliation can be effected. But is this really evident? If ever the pastor dares to come up with an idea pointing in this direction, he risks dismissal or alienation from the congregation. If the pastor wants to live in a simple house in a rich neighbourhood, his parishioners will be upset because it lowers the prestige of their church. In a newly built area the church building is planned together with the mall and the schools, imprisoned in the urban planning design; how can the church not reflect the walks of life of the people around? Is there a way to break down inner barricades? How is this problem felt in a rich neighbourhood?

I decided to speak about it with one of the pastors at St Luke's Lutheran Church in Park Ridge. At first I hesitated. The hesitation sprang from my own uncertainty: why do I feel a certain aggressiveness when I walk on the plush carpets of a suburban church and see the fancy couches and elegant lampstands in the rooms where the clergy welcome their penitents? Am I so sure that I know and live the reality of the Gospel? Is the Gospel not like an immense horizon on which I can distinguish only some distant points, and does not everyone else discover other insights that are important to him or to her and based on the same reference as are my own perceptions? Am I not 'sectarian' by recognizing in voluntary poverty a strong sign of the radical nature of the Gospel? The worker priests in France could become so totally interested in the working class and the poor because they had either their own middle-class background or their sophisticated seminary education behind them. If certain religious orders have emphasized so much the necessity of living out poverty among the poor, did they not choose that direction knowing they were taking only one aspect out of Christ's life, perhaps a hitherto neglected one? The Jesuits possess universities, colleges, investment portfolios and endowments, and would I say they reflect the way of the Gospel less? Or is it true that each age has to answer the demands of the Gospel in the context of the problems of its own day? And is the problem of our age not the disparity of rich and poor throughout the whole world? Is it not true that the young generations, from the sixties on, with their fresh look at the world as they discovered it, insisted on the sharing of material goods, on the breaking of barriers between people and on the oneness of the people of God?

The pastor agrees that there is a great need for the Church to foster reconciliation between Park Ridge's segment of society and the segments that are within the boundaries of Chicago. He mentions the emptiness in the lives of many and the problems due to the social stratification that exists even here between the newcomers and those who have been living in the community for a long time. Some families are regarded as socially prominent. There had just been a minor conflict in the parish with one of those families. They wanted the Christmas tree up for their daughter's wedding. She always dreamt of a wedding in a Christmas setting. The story indicates the kind of little crises that can cause ripples in the still water of a well-to-do parish. But the example is basically to illustrate this question: how to maintain an attitude of faith, and faithfulness, to the Gospel while still providing a good pastoral ministry? How to maintain openness of communication without compromising what faith is all about? How to proclaim the Gospel, to live the Gospel and to maintain a way of life in the congregation which is as consistent with the Gospel as possible? For example, people in the parish recently clashed over the question of catechetical instruction. In years gone by students preparing for Confirmation had only to go to class. You could go to class for two years and never set foot in the church on Sunday morning and still be confirmed. The new clergy has emphasized worship, revamping the catechetical programme in such a way that worship becomes an essential part of it. The theory behind this is that Confirmation means affirming one's baptismal promises and that therefore this has to take place in the context of the Body. What else would it be? Maybe an orientation or a learning experience, a doctrinal class, but not a spiritual experience, a deepening, or a spiritual development. Because of this insistence on the integration of the catechism into the worshipping community, the parish lost five families. In the face of emptiness, of an attitude that treats the Church as just another social institution, as a place of non-commitment, the clergy here wanted to centre everything on spiritual development and formation, part of which means sharing with the worshipping community. Young people have all-night vigils. Evangelical ministers come to their retreats. A doctrine class for adults helps people to articulate their faith and to grow towards spiritual depth.

'What do you pray for, in regard to your parish?', I ask the Park Ridge Lutheran pastor. The first answer is a joke: 'We pray for money'. But then comes another answer. He prays for a new openness to the activity of the Spirit. That in that openness there might be spiritual, emotional growth and that the whole person might grow and do so in such a way that reconciliation might become effective. He prays for healing, healing of the wounds that society inflicts, that individuals inflict upon themselves. The anger he sees in so many people is not just anger directed at others or at society but anger with themselves because they have failed and have not become whom they were told they should become. Recently, at a 'bureaucratic' meeting, called Parish Life Committee, he took part in a learning experience about spiritual formation. That meeting ended with an evening prayer and an anointing service. The participants could come to him or another person and request prayer; then, they would kneel and he would simply place both hands on their heads and pray for whatever they requested. If they made no requests, he could simply pray for what he believed they were in need of. He was astounded by the desire for healing manifested on that occasion. This desire exists so much in people. He prays for healing in the personal brokenness but also in the corporate brokenness that sensitive people feel. It is a way of forming people of communion, people marked by the challenge of reconciliation wherever they are, people who are able to listen. In a city like Chicago so many will not listen. Where can you be heard? Therefore, all of us who are part of the Church must remind ourselves of the source, our need for the sustenance by the Spirit. We have to see beyond our desire for self-aggrandizement, acknowledge our brokenness while developing our willingness to heal and to listen.

On my way back to Chicago, I wonder why I'm somehow disappointed with the answers that were given. First of all, I say to myself, I came with too many questions. If you travel through a city, from one neighbourhood to another, the global questions come to you all at once. People are impressed by their own powerlessness and compulsion that thrives on resignation. The problems are so immense that people react in order to protect themselves with: let's at least focus on the small scale of my immediate neighbours where I know everybody. Secondly, I remember that I, too, expected decisive answers. I did not consider the brokenness of the church, its helplessness, no matter how rich it may be, how many means it may have. In many areas, the Church is not able to give immediate, definite answers. Its task is simply to make the Gospel present as much as possible, here and now, to immerse people in it, to let it work in the souls of human beings where so much is in constant struggle and turmoil, and to keep the Gospel of forgiveness and reconciliation, of repentance and love of enemy high above the heads of the people. The deacon in the Orthodox liturgy does this when he carries the Holy Book high above us as a beacon and as a refuge, whenever we happen to drift down into resignation and hopelessness. All the spiritual development, the retreats, the worship and the catechism, the Christmas tree during Advent, the healing and the anointing, and the prayer for openness to the Spirit converge to place, in the emptiness of our superficial lives, the fullness of the Gospel. And if we ourselves are not capable of radiating reconciliation around us, will that Gospel in the end not begin to shine beyond ourselves and become the eye-opener so that people who are opposed and divided can come to themselves, can come together?

Seventy times seven churches . . .
Who knows exactly the differences between Wesleyan Methodists and Southern Baptists, between Missouri Synod Lutherans and Christian Reformed, between Billy Graham and Robert Schuller? Would it be of help if scholars came up with a new classification, a typology of churches? Could seventy times seven churches be simplified to seven types of churches, each of them emphasizing one or the other aspect of what the universal Church was meant to be? Many Churches were started out of opposition to a mother Church in which institutional routine led to the neglect of a truth now considered as the most essential or the only valid one. People were fascinated by an insight concerning the mystery of Christ — justification, sanctification, predestination — missed this new emphasis in their own church, and walked away with it, proclaiming the kingdom of God in their own way.

The Catholic Church has been able at different moments of its history to contain centrifugal movements, through the biasing detour of religious orders and congregations. Franciscans perceived Christ in the first place as the poor and suffering servant, Dominicans as the teaching master, Benedictines as the praying high priest, but they all have been conscious of selecting only a fragment out of the totality of Christ's life. Their members recognized the same image of the living Christ and accomplished, by following

141

'their' Christ, a ministry *within* the whole Church. They became an avant garde, a dynamic force in the mother Church. In general, they became themselves, earlier or later, institutionalized movements, awakened periodically by new stirrings. In Protestantism, renewal movements often have preferred to move out, or they have been obliged to leave in order to shape in an exclusive way the ideal fellowship of Christ. This dramatic evolution rests on the principle of division that had been the option of the Reformation in the sixteenth century. The confusing and hypocritical diversity in Protestantism is the recurring part of a decimal fraction that was started at the beginning of the modern era. Since then, the Church has exploded, cutting itself off from its own roots and drifting away in countless movements, all partial, one-sided and limited, forgetting after some time the very bonds that link them with the Church they separated from as well as the existing unity as God's gift. Since then the vision of the Church has been vague: does God first call people as individuals who then have to organize a church? Is the Church a purely spiritual community or an institution of faith, forms and structures? Is the Church divided into a visible and an invisible part, the latter being holy and the former partial and entangled in sin and deficiency? Is the Church the body of Christ or a human institution, hidden from the eyes of the world but visible to the eyes of faith?

Has this evolution been stimulated on the American shores because of the new democratization that replaced the old European 'Christian' order of society with its authorities and hierarchies? Has the continuous founding of new churches been precipitated by a nineteenth century vision of humanity, free from original sin, a myth of innocence for people without a past who have only a future in common? Were divisions simply perpetuating themselves because the willingness to transform society toward the Kingdom asked for ever new adaptations of the church body, irreconcilable with the institutionalized denominations? Even between

Evangelicals unity does not exist and doesn't seem longed for. In transdenominational evangelicalism built around networks of parachurch agencies, the structure — says George Marshden from Calvin College, Grand Rapids — is somewhat like that of the feudal system of the Middle Ages: 'It is made up of superficially friendly, somewhat competitive, empires built up by evangelists competing for the same audiences, but all professing allegiance to the same king.' But then, where is the Church?

Any new classification of churches will have to confront another question. How many people do identify themselves completely with the official doctrine, style and structure of their own church? People easily switch from one denomination to another. Certain Catholics speak to you more often with a vocabulary derivated from Jimmy Swaggart than from Pope John Paul II. On the other hand, a common mind can be found across confessional lines through ecumenical dialogue, so people start to belong to different traditions. Should that be regarded as confusion or as a fruit of ecumenism, a beginning of the uniting between churches?

I have a hunch that a typology of American churches could show the complementary emphases churches have stressed: either on liturgy and celebration, on spirituality and inner life, on 'monastic' values, on neighbourhood and community, on mission, on peace and justice, on revival, renewal, and aggiornamento. The monastic tradition is not absent from American Protestantism, because Wesley, Zinzendorf, and Bonhoeffer, who have had such a huge influence on the American scene, all have been fascinated by some monastic tradition. Two young adults, raised in the Reformed Church of America and the Christian Reformed Church, both distinctly 'non-monastic' churches, told me that in their opinion the Christian monastic tradition has had as its goals both to offer training in the full appropriation and realization of our dependence on God and to live a life formed by the expression of this realization of God's centrality and our utter dependence. They added that training

143

in the realization of God's centrality and a life that expresses this realization sketch out the general direction of their own vocational groping and that, therefore, the monastic tradition has something important to do with their vocation. They were thinking about living without provisions, because when one recognizes that one is without provisions, without reserves in storage, then one sees that it is God, and God alone, who gives us all things. It seems to me that, not only the Shakers and the Mennonites, or the original Wesleyan class-system, the Moravian bands and the Awakening movements, or the Quakers and the Sojourners with their 'community of communities', but also the core groups in many mainline parishes have kept vestiges of that monastic tradition, including groups in the farthest corners of Evangelicalism, especially in their 'inner-worldly asceticism'.

There are networks of peace and justice groups across the country and across churches. In a chancery room in San Francisco, archdiocesan leaders shared with me their dream of basic Christian communities, where the justice issues would be woven into the liturgical life of the congregation. These basic communities would involve people from different parishes and parishes from other denominational bodies, focusing first on the nuclear issue but later on other issues as well. This will be the option for the future: acting at the grassroots, gathering communities, getting around the pastors until they come along somehow, rebuilding the church starting from social justice concerns. Already now, there is ecumenical information sharing, there are newsletters and sharing about strategies for how to enter the parish community. For instance, it is harder to break into the parishes of any denomination with the Latin American issue, but with the help of the wedge of the nuclear issue, a breakthrough has been made. The peace education issue focuses on the parish because the leaders see it as a marvellous organizational unit for their purposes. Religious congregations of women in each community also have a

144

social justice co-ordinator. They meet together regularly and are the central means of communication to all the Sisters who very often have more immediate contacts with the people in the parishes than the pastor and who are freer in many ways.

I mentioned to the archdiocesan leaders that the New York archdiocese has a commission on spiritual development for the priests and another one for the laity. Would it be possible to imagine a similar initiative in San Francisco, with people running around from parish to parish, renewing what they can, opening up relationships with other Catholic and non-Catholic parishes? Is there enthusiasm in the social justice field because it is new, because there are resistances, because you work on issues related to immediate needs? Why is there not the same rebuilding of the church on other levels? And would such an effort not bear fruit on the level of evangelization and not sharpen, sustain and stimulate the involvement in situations of social injustice? There is no committee or division quite like that. They think it is bad theology to have a special spiritual development. Are they still part of that generation that has analyzed the lack of authenticity of a church, which by emphasizing spiritual values, neglected the commitment to the poor and amalgamated itself with the bourgeois values of society? Is real spirituality not subversive? They say there is a deep prayer component in the reflection-action groups. 'The ability to pray together in the midst of actions is extremely *useful* in helping people work through their anxieties and anger.' Is prayer an auxiliary aspect of social justice and liberation? Or has it its own finality as a priority and as the nerve of everything else? But they say that spiritual development is in the method and comes out of it. Within this method, for instance, liturgical celebrations are planned.

A typology of church emphases would help us to see that we need all the other expressions, that liturgy and inner life, covenant among ourselves and community issues, mission and peace and justice, and renewal and revival all are

145

aspects of church life and should be present in each local church. It is all one church; all of these expressions belong to the ministry of the church in spite of the walls that separate us and prevent us from becoming a visible reconciled church in the face of the world around us.

A dynamic of unity instead of division

One of Niebuhr's conclusions, reflecting upon ways to unity, states that 'the road to unity is the road of sacrifice which asks of churches as of individuals that they lose their lives in order that they may find the fulfilment of their better selves'. In order to become a reconciling community of believers, the believers, as persons and as Churches, need to reconcile themselves, to turn around self-exalting justifications, and to lose themselves by entering into a dynamic of unity instead of division. How can Churches call people to come together in mutual love, if Christians themselves show the image of a chaotically, often fanatically divided Body? How can churches be places of forgiveness, if Christians themselves don't want to accept one another and don't find ways to share what is at the very heart of their being together: the life of Christ? They belong together. To deny that as a Black Baptist I need the Irish Catholics and as a Fundamentalist the high church Episcopalians, and vice versa, means denying our very belonging to Christ, the variety of his gifts, given to build up his Body for the salvation of the whole human family.

I'm standing on the balcony of a high-rise building south of Thirty-first street in Chicago. Because of the mist, I can't see very far. Several other high-rises stand out in the mist: a landscape of giant geometrical ghosts uplifted in mystical levitation. Developers have adorned them with the most lovely bucolic names, dreamy epithets contrasting with the shriek of urban compression and destitution. Some of the worst slums once stood here. Now people walk through the anonymous overheated corridors like through underground tunnels; this no man's land they pass through as quickly as

146

possible, before catching their breath again, in the freedom of their individual space. People are seduced by the view overlooking the lake. But the views to the west and to the south show a sea of poverty ebbing away from their feet.

To the south I observe some areas of renewal. Urban renewal is coming up north from Hyde Park, the academic area, through Kenwood which still looks tremendously poor but where some beginnings of renovation are being undertaken. The same thing is true for the area immediately south of the Lake Meadows building, from Thirty-first to Thirty-fifth Street. The poor are between Thirty-fifth and Forty-seventh Streets in public housing. To the west over towards the Dan Ryan Expressway are the Robert Taylor Homes, one mile and a half of public housing for thirty thousand people and one of the largest housing projects in Chicago. The complex makes a very sad impression, and the stories one hears about life in those buildings are as bad as those about Cabrini Green on the North Side. Some high-rises down on the monumental Dr Martin Luther King Drive indicate that inroads are being made into the poverty area; many of those buildings are for senior citizens and are subsidized by government money. Close by old mansions are being rehabilitated now. The streets look like a lumber yard; families are moving in, buying up the old homes and putting in a lot of work with the intention of living in them for years. It is an example of black gentrification. Neighbourhood residents in this gentrified area are vigilant about the upkeep of the area, encourage people who move in to work on their buildings, are very concerned about the kind of stores that go in and are opposed to liquor stores that could become hangouts. The aim is to keep out the people from the public housing area, especially the drug addicts and winos who hang out along Thirty-fifth Street. Both are black neighbourhoods. Humanity's poverty, competition, disillusionment, despair and separation, in a microcosm, seen from a panoramic viewpoint . . . Jesus wept over the city.

I went to Christ the Mediator, a Lutheran church. Eighty per cent of the members of this church live within a mile radius, the majority of them being single people, unmarried or divorced. They have only six families, and some single-parent families. Seventy per cent of the congregation is black. Economically speaking, the members tend to be middle-class professional people who work downtown, a few minutes away. A few people come from the perimeters, either upper-class who live on the lake shore behind the high-rises or lower-class who live in the public housing areas. The liturgical life as well as a warm sense of hospitality attract people from elsewhere. Often they bring the economic wherewithal the congregation needs. It is Thanksgiving weekend, so middle-class America is criss-crossing the country (in a society of leisure the number of Sundays in the course of the year on which people are not travelling, skiing, sailing or visiting friends becomes more and more limited). At Christ the Mediator at the beginning of the service, more than half of the congregation disappear into the chancel in order to fulfil the different roles of the liturgy. The service looks like a rehearsal, with all the actors up front and some star gazers and loungers in the nave waiting for something to happen. Since the roles are so obviously divided among the crowd in the chancel, and the rest of the church remains practically empty, the whole problem of liturgical participation, so much debated in ministerial meetings, doesn't exist any more. The pastor tells me that at a baptism the whole congregation just marches to the font, though no one has ever told them to do so. They just get up and go. They follow the cross and crowd down in there. During the parish announcements at the end, the last liturgical act together, everybody has to turn around on the non-movable pews to face the exit in order to listen to the chancel group. The pastor thinks that the aggressiveness about their doing of liturgy, this robustness, is an American cultural influence on a liturgical form that in itself is very traditional and not different from what people in Sweden or Germany would do.

148

On the corner of the same street, I had noticed a big church called Olivet Baptist Church. It was once a congregation of ten thousand people, but is now down to about three thousand. In this area, like in so many other places, one of the problems is trying to build bridges between the old mainline denominations, that is to say the more Catholic-type or liturgical churches (Episcopalian, Lutheran, Roman Catholic, Eastern Orthodox) and those which sometimes predominate in a black community, especially Baptist and Pentecostal churches. They have imaginative names painted on their storefronts and actively evangelize and attempt to build large congregations. While the more Catholic churches are able to count on support from their sister-churches in the suburbs, these congregations have to be able to support the preachers. It is one of the vulnerable aspects of the splintering and splitting of the church into congregationalism. Is that one of the reasons why Olivet is not involved in any kind of neighbourhood renewal? On the other hand, in most cases the more Catholic churches don't make a big effort to reach the evangelical churches either or to find the level on which they would be able to co-operate. Why bother to try? An attitude of resignation prevails as if the distance between them is too far, while in reality so many essential values are common to both traditions. It certainly requires a firm faith in the unity of the Church, spiritual discernment, a capacity to admire and the intelligence of a serpent to cross the bridge and not to stop half-way and return home where everything is neat and known. What examples of such bridges are here? In this area in Chicago, there is not even a clergy association which would give the ministers at least a structure for their meetings. Over on Wabash I see the large steeple of St James, a Catholic parish. They have a social ministry largely staffed by the nuns. Their food pantry is helped by Christ the Mediator, which collects food every month and takes it over to St James. The Little Brothers of the Poor use the parish facilities of an Episcopal church in the area as a senior citizens' centre. That is all. Even between the mainline denominations there are not many links. The Lutheran churches have at least decided to reflect their neighbourhoods; logically, this should lead them one day to envisage a relationship with the other churches in the area and to pursue an ecumenical ministry.

What can I learn in Chicago about the rift between the old mainline churches and the congregations that predominate in black communities? The first thing is that not all the blacks — almost fifty per cent in the city of Chicago — are members of Baptist, Pentecostal or Methodist churches. Often there are purely black denominations like the African Methodist Episcopal church, an off-shoot of the Methodist Church. Yet it is true that many blacks come from Baptist and Methodist backgrounds. These were the denominations that were active in the South. The Methodist circuit riders and the Baptist preachers were there; they had the missionary dash. Also, those preachers didn't have to care about hierarchy, prayer books or ecclesiastical structures, because there they were, sole representatives of the Gospel, sure of the personal call they had heard to preach and to gather a group of people around themselves for the development of church life. In what was the new South in those early days of the country — parts of Georgia, Alabama, Mississippi as well as Tennessee, Kentucky, Louisiana and Texas — the Evangelical groups were the churches that grew among the black slave population. On the other hand, there were many black Catholics in areas where the Roman Catholic church was strong — in New Orleans, around Baltimore, Cincinnati, Louisville, and St Louis. Episcopalians, Presbyterians, and Missouri Synod Lutherans also had pockets of growth in the South. But the Baptists and Methodists were omnipresent. If historically the free churches have appealed more to blacks, it is certainly due in part to the fact that those denominations were strong right there and invested their missionary zeal. This doesn't mean that liturgical churches were, or would have to be, less

150

attractive to them. There was certainly a compatibility between the black experience of oppression and discrimination and the Anabaptist churches that originated in revolts against the establishment in Europe. The irony of their history is that in America, the free church tradition became the major religious expression and was no longer the expression of a suppressed minority like in Europe. Immigrants, Puritans, pietists, Wesleyan revivalists, Baptists and all of the others built up established churches in America. On the other hand, the immigrants' origins of oppression must have profoundly moulded the shape of their faith and piety, for instance in disposing them to a much more emotional expression of religion than the liturgical churches could offer. Those churches that cultivated an emotional style of worship and an effervescent church life were more likely to touch people who were themselves under oppression. The cultural situation in America was a different one from the free churches, but their origins of oppression, their emotional style of piety and their missionary zeal made them close to the blacks.

I come from a tradition of Reformed Protestantism in which rational intelligibility made possible by much preaching, exegetical explanation and dogmatic thinking became a priority, although we sang the beautiful sixteenth century hymns with tears in our eyes. But in other mainline denominations, especially in the inner cities, one can now find a liturgical style that emphasizes more the Catholic than the Protestant heritage. The liturgical churches have kept a treasure of symbols: they lay on hands, they anoint, they spread incense and sprinkle water, they offer silence; they allow people to kneel, to dance, to stand up, to prostrate, they initiate; they celebrate a sacrifice and they dress in white or in varying colours. The liturgical churches seem to be attractive to people in general who, in a super-technological world, become more attentive to, and have need of, those profound and age-old symbols that reach into the subconscious history of humankind. It seems to me that black people in particular, as well as Hispanics, are even more sensitive to that longing for transcendence that inhabits the human heart and that their cultures, however much they may have been transformed by conquering civilizations that saw them as archaic and primitive, honour more deeply the religious dimension of the whole of life. For many others, wounded by life, by the conditions of living, the depths of guilt, the horror of incurable illness, calamity and death, ritual and liturgy are a remedy. Others who no longer have a blind faith in 'secular' therapy become attentive to that realm of symbols which is at the heart of the Church in its oldest Catholic and Eastern Orthodox traditions.

In a certain sense the more 'Catholic' churches have kept up a corporate spirituality, a sense of the universality of the Church, a sense of communion through the liturgy which, in the non-Catholic churches, is a residue of the Catholic substance. Some would say that many Catholics themselves have lost a lot of that. Luther was able to risk a reformation and separation from the existing Church because he found in himself another understanding of faith that was opposed to the faith of the church of his time. Later, in Lutheranism, in Anglicanism and perhaps in some Calvinistic currents as well, through the liturgy and the music, the Catholic substance could surface again. On the other hand, it is often said that the seeds sown in the late Middle Ages by all kinds of reform movements amid all the social, cultural, economic and political changes that were going on, nurtured by the Renaissance and the Reformation, came to a full flowering in the more radical elements of the Reformation, for instance among the Anabaptists and the Puritans in England. These were the people who came to the United States in great numbers, seeking religious freedom. Among the Lutherans many pietists came. No wonder that an individualistic piety became so prevalent. The dimension of the mystical body of Christ was strange to them. Also, the free churches that came to America have absorbed passively, and modelled actively, the whole culture. They immersed themselves in the culture that was beginning to take shape. The more radical elements of the Reformation have influenced the birth and development of capitalism and industrialization. The last wave of the European immigration was the Eastern Europeans, Ukranians, Russians, and Yugoslavians. They are still first and second generation. They have created cohesive ethnic neighbourhoods, a sense of belonging, and a sense of communal understanding. They have kept the Orthodox liturgy with all its richness. If they don't become completely indigenized into the American culture, will they be able to communicate to the other Churches their gifts, the richness of a church that derives all its life and radiance from the holy liturgy? Here and there one sees, already now, an Orthodox influence: icons adorn the corner of a room or a chapel, litanies are sung, and priests and parishioners move around together during the service. I remember an evening prayer in New Orleans to which many priests and religious came. Normally they have to be in charge of everything at celebrations. Here they could simply sit down without being looked at, stare at the ascending smoke of the candles, listen to the vocalizing sounds of alternately sweet and strong voices and plunge with nostalgia into the silence of their own heart. Moreover, the exceptional blend of styles, with Eastern-Orthodox characteristics dominating, opened them up to another dimension than their daily running around in the rat-race of commitments, meetings and prayer services. There a religious woman discovered inside of her, deep down, the passion for holiness that will not go away or let itself be suppressed, the longing for the Kingdom to be built up here and now, the energy for God. For her the evening prayer was not only a peaceful time of leisure before God but also a moment of strengthened hope. A hope, she wrote me the next day, which is 'not in head, heart, or stomach; it is the interlocking of all three, beyond dreaming, imagining, reasoning, feeling, yet composed of all the dreams-images-reasons-feeling I carry inside of me. A hope which pulls all these together and propels me to make meaning of my life now'.

Ways of unity can be opened as soon as we realize that we need the gifts of the others, recognize that their gifts are gifts of God, and enrich ourselves with them. Billy Graham once said that we need, after our first conversion to Christ, a second one through which we are sent back to the world. As Christians we all are in a transitional stage. Some go through a very personal kind of individual conversion; all their energy, love, and attachment is focused on this primordial experience. Maybe only later will they experience the depth and richness of being part of a rich heritage of generations of Christians, of a community of people who transmitted the Gospel from old to young, from neighbour to neighbour, on death-beds and in concentration camps, behind prison gates and on journeys thousands of miles from home. A part of what is missing for the evangelical who experiences his conversion is the Catholic heritage and tradition. Another part of what is missing is a responsibility for the rest of the world. But old churches don't change anymore in many places; they fail to speak to genuine emotions, they don't connect their faith with the heart. Many Catholics are drawn to fundamentalist or Pentecostal groups because there the people are alive, they do social work, they pick up old ladies in vans on Sunday, they love the poor, they pray, visit the sick, organize missions and have a spirituality of raising hands, speaking in tongues, of enthusiasm that contrasts with the sedate, rational, uniform old Catholic style. Because we have institutionalized the scandal of disunity and developed mentalities, belief systems and organizational structures in opposition to others, we have forgotten our common belonging. Now it is only by penetrating behind the divisions that we can rediscover the mystery of unity given by God to his Church. Especially over the past five hundred years, in a purist search for the holiness of the Church, we have been estranged from one another. Being born out of a divorce, we were tempted to repeat a divorce in our own life. Our mother churches have not been able to keep us at home because of our urge to drift away and to start from scratch. Somebody walked away with an idea about God and started a new Church. The Catholic Church of the thirteenth century was still able to integrate renewal movements by giving them a place as religious orders. The Church of England of the eighteenth century lost Wesley and the Methodists, although they did not want to leave and called their meeting places 'chapel', 'preaching house' and not 'church'. Charismatics often give the impression of cutting themselves off from the institutional church by starting another one, rooted in a particular spirituality, bringing together people from the established parishes, loosening the sense of the universal Church. They sometimes revive the old dichotomy between the freedom of the Spirit and the old church structure in which it is supposedly impossible to live out their spiritual gifts. But it seems that, in the face of a possible Protestantization of the Catholic Charismatic movement, a repetition of what has happened to Methodism in the Church of England has been avoided. Today Christians of all kinds are invited to choose for a new inclusiveness rather than to perpetuate the old exclusions. The ecumenical movement has not been able to stop the dynamics of division. According to the *World Christian Encyclopedia* (Oxford University Press, 1982) nineteen hundred denominations existed at the beginning of this century; today they are twenty two thousand. Each week five new denominations start anew. Are we ready to enter into a dynamic of reconciliation? Are we ready to reverse the trends toward further divisions? Are we ready to embody together whatever we will discover as treasures of faith and hope and love among other Christians? I know a young man who had to visit his family in Australia and New Zealand and who decided to take with him a paschal candle. On his way he visited with communities, parishes, monasteries, families and, in each place, he began by lighting the candle he had carried on his back. 'Christ is risen', he said, 'This candle is a sign of the unity I would like to celebrate with you'.

One day I entered the sanctuary of Fourth Presbyterian Church on North Michigan Avenue in Chicago. I looked around for a cross, and somehow missed it. But then my eyes discerned in the dark, high above the chancel, a stained-glass window depicting the risen Christ with his arms outstretched. I thought how much we need to look towards him beyond all the political allegiances and designations, economic and intellectual differences, ethnic or racial belongings that divide the churches. I heard the preacher saying that Jesus is the great denominator of life, the answer to all our needs and that all find their ideal in him. 'To the banker he is the hidden treasure, to the baker the bread of life, to the florist the lily of the valley, to the geologist the rock of ages, to the jeweller the pearl of great price, to the carpenter the door of heaven, to the thirsty the water of life, to the hungry the bread of life, to the (here I understood "psychologist", but it doesn't sound good enough!) the light of life, to the lost the Saviour.' It is all true but he is also beyond all that, lifted up high above the chancel, far beyond our need of appropriating him, in the unity of the Father and the Spirit, existing in God's own love, the only source of reconciliation in the human family.

A Litany of Belonging

Jesus, Gate of praise,
who offers an opening in the maze of human despair
to unite the lost with those who live,
by your Incarnation
you knock at the door in anticipation of our longing.
— We shall see you face to face!

Jesus, Light of life,
who will brighten, when sought alone
and transform loneliness into joyful trust,
by your Transfiguration
you reveal to us the horizon of our journey.
— We shall see you face to face!

Jesus, Image of compassion,
who descends into the abyss of the human condition
to accompany those who daily need a new beginning,
by your Passion
you brand us with the innocence of your forgiveness.
— We shall see you face to face!

Jesus, eternal Love,
who trembles before the death of humankind
and comes to smite death and fill with life,
by your Resurrection
you deliver us into your boundless love.
— We shall see you face to face!

Jesus, River of living water,
who rises to meet us on our abandoned shores,
and so cultivates a new land,
by the Spirit of promise
you raise abundant harvests for your people.
— We shall see you face to face!

How to Use *Belonging* on Retreat or in Discussion Groups

A retreat is a moment of vacation during which we put aside the newspaper, cancel appointments, and ask ourselves in our innermost heart: "God, what is the meaning of all this? What is really going on, underneath all the events I'm involved in? To whom does my life matter? Who listens to me? What are the gifts in me that you want me to use? To whom should my life matter?" No retreat is possible without a certain alarm and even despair, without the awareness of some incongruity in one's own life. This is also the reason why a time of retreat is not necessarily immediately, instantly a nice time. At least by taking time out—and by losing it—do we dare to stop, trying to tear down artificial walls of self-protection and opening out to God. Discordant voices may still persecute us, but as we quietly persevere and come back over and over again to ourselves, some truth about the unique person we are and some truth about God will emerge.

Retreats can be held anywhere. On an airplane most people don't have a schedule of activities and can find the leisure between meals and movies to stare out into the clouds. Many people listen to a cassette of quiet music in their cars, as a way of shutting off automatic thoughts and of entering into prayer. I know an engineer who dances every day all by himself to the rhythms of Pergolese's *Stabat Mater*. A mother of three children takes one whole night of prayer every month. You see people in conference centers walking all day up and down corridors, in silent reflection, like monks-for-a-day rotating in circular cloisters. There are thousands of retreat houses with upper rooms, chapels, kneelers, and miles of silence. Ministers have hideouts in their garages, where they are alone with only books, piled up or decorating the walls, as witnesses to their intimate wrestling.

Retreats can last a minute or thirty days. They can be done alone or with others. They may take place when you feel down or when you are in seventh heaven. But every retreat has to do with the longing to belong . . .

First step. Aim: to remember to whom you belong. Start your retreat with a biblical reading, for instance, John 15: "I am the true vine. . . . Dwell in me, as I in you. . . . Apart from me you can do nothing. . . . Dwell in my love." Or make a list of titles given to Jesus by John's Gospel, such as "I am the good shepherd," "I am the light," and find out what you would like to call Jesus, deep within yourself. Or take a psalm—like Psalm 63, 103, or 139—and translate it in your own words, in your own most personal language, until the psalm becomes a prayer in you that comes from the heart. Only then ask yourself, in a spirit of prayer, questions like: What does it mean for me to belong to God? Before whom do I live my life? How can I dwell in Christ's love, at the center of my life? Am I ready to abandon myself so that this love becomes more and more the core of my existence, personally and in my relationships with others, in my responsibilities and in my choices?

In a discussion group—be it the Sunrise Saints in Sacramento, California, who meet for prayer and breakfast, or an Episcopal vestry in Copperas Cove, Texas, who read together one book a month, or a "root-group" of volunteers living together for one year among poor people in Orlando, Florida—the same questions may be asked. It is wise, however, to start together with a time of silence lasting ten to twenty minutes during which people are invited to take notes individually. Don't split up during this silence; stay all together. It is also important to agree on a certain style: sharing is first of all a listening experience; long monologues oppress the others; impulsive reactions destroy whatever you have treasured up in your own heart.

Second step. While reading "Fourteen Stations on a Way of Belonging," focus on these two statements made in the introduction: "Only by suffering with those who suffer are we able to abandon ourselves and to recognize the silhouette of Another on the horizon of our destination" and "As soon as we let go the tyranny of self and, in stillness, discover the Suffering Servant present in the human family, all the dimensions of belonging, as in reflecting mirrors, break open."

159

Do you agree? Are there people in your family or around you whose burdens you would like to lay down at the foot of the cross? You notice that you can't live as if your neighbor's suffering didn't exist: somehow their burdens concern you; somehow their burdens are your burdens. But we are frightened, and we don't know how to be present to people who suffer. There is, however, the cross: God carries in Christ all humanity's burdens. How can we, despite our fragility and fears, extend the width of our arms to those who are suffering so as to enter into Christ's own work of salvation and transfiguration?

If several small groups meet simultaneously, each one of them may be invited to prepare an intercession expressing the main concern of the small group members. The intercessions of all the groups may be brought into the worship or eucharist at the end of the day.

Third step. The chapter "Carrying Each Other" starts by saying that if we recognize in people's suffering a reflection of God's self offering love, we discover in ourselves the gift of solidarity. "It is there, although most of the time it is buried, concealed, and forgotten. We have to let it rise again." How can we uncover in ourselves this gift and let it flow throughout our daily activities? Do you know people in whom this gift becomes visible? How do these unsung saints go about it? They don't impress you because of their spectacular activities, but because of their simplicity, of the transparency of their love. Do they seem to be super-human? If not, how can you find in yourself that same gift of solidarity? What is your personal ministry? And very concretely, what could be your next step? Take a step within your reach, however simple it may seem to be. Later you will notice that you found—how, you don't know (Mark 4:27)—the courage to believe in your own vocation to carry others. Belonging is life-giving.

Would you agree with the conclusion of this chapter: "Others are part of yourself." "You are married to humanity." "No one is only himself or herself"?

Fourth step. In *Listening to People of Hope* (1984) I spoke about the preparation of a "pilgrimage of reconciliation," still going on, that allowed me to discover many signs of hope, often hidden ones. In each town the preparation is a grassroots effort, building on what has already been accomplished by local groups and individuals without trying to take on a fixed structure or function as an "alternative" organization. Instead, this preparation consists in visits to churches that are trying to live out in prayer and worship and life the gospel's implications and to neighborhood organizations whose concrete efforts, often through long-term political struggle, seek to remedy local problems. These visits encourage and cement networking between many people, perhaps previously unknown to one another, who share the same convictions and commitments, hopes, and dreams. The challenge can be felt: if others are doing so much, perhaps with limited resources, what are we doing? Thus a pilgrimage is not a single event, but a period of "walking together" that does not end with one evening or one weekend of celebration and sharing. The effects can be perceived in individuals whose horizons have been widened, in church communities in which the connection between authentic prayer and concrete work for reconciliation in justice are perceived, and in local organizations who benefit from the exchange of ideas and commitments formed through discovering grassroots groups and individuals previously unknown.

In chapters 3 and 4 of *Belonging* I describe a certain number of initiatives that I've encountered, all centered around this challenge of building up community and reconciling Chrisitan churches. I believe that as soon as we have received deep within ourselves the contemplative gift of belonging, we feel the urge to leave our own preoccupations and the drive to build up community wherever we are and revive the church in the spirit of reconciliation.

How can I join others to build up, creatively, community among my neighbors, in my locality, town, or region? How does my parish or congregation relate to existing neighborhood organizations? Could the interpenetration between parish and neighborhood be a way of expressing the gift of belonging to God and the human family in a concrete way? When I look around in my community, do I see signs of hope? What ways do I see for giving my community, my area, my city, a soul? How can we become catalysts of justice amid the brokenness of the poor? Is it not in the community of the disciples of Christ that the poor can discover hope, because nowhere except in Christ are barriers between people broken down? Can the Christian communities in your neighborhood, by discovering their specific and complementary gifts of ministry, become "a network, a framework, a chain of relations, links of love which are capable of supporting so many other people"?

Fifth step. But our efforts will be vain if we don't restore love among ourselves, if the church does not become what it is called to be: the body of Christ, a place of reconciliation, an authenthic community of people who all belong together. How can we change our way of looking at other Christians, viewing them not with anxiety or in a spirit of competition, but seeing them with inner peace, becoming aware of their gifts? How can we become reconcilers and discover the gifts God has given to the various Christian traditions? Chapter 4 is a call to the American churches. How do you see the church? How can you open ways of unity?

Recently, in Pasadena, California, I asked all these questions during a pilgrimage. After a few moments of silence somebody stood up and said:

Ask, and it shall be given. . . . May the church be a place of refreshment and renewal, a green garden of quiet fragrant flowers and whispering trees, its beauty in its *being*, not in its *doing*. May the church be a listening place, a place to whisper hopes, shout joys, cry sorrows—without condemnation, only eyes meeting eyes, a smile, a gentle embrace, words of comfort. May the church be a place that honors all persons—not because of anything they can do, but simply because they are. May the church be a haven for the forgotten, the misunderstood, the lost—where sins are forgiven, doubts can be aired, mistakes admitted, failures overlooked. May the church be a celebration—of music, candles, fragrance, colors, rejoicing in the gifts that everyone can bring—gifts of happiness, understanding. May the church be a river: carrying life, shining in the sun, washing us clean, giving us a place for our longing, a place to belong.